# IN THE I

## A Cape Breton Coal Miner

*IN THE PIT: A Cape Breton Coal Miner* is a rare, exciting insider's story of coal mine life. There are no strikes or explosions here—just the gripping drama and rich good humour of one man's daily work underground, from the brute shoveling at the coal face and hand-shifting tons of shaker pans, to hurling through low, narrow tunnels testing a diesel during early mechanization. You are not spared the details.

Rennie MacKenzie worked fifteen years in 12 and 18 Collieries, New Waterford. Then he left the mines, went to college, and served as a United Church minister. He has retired to New Waterford, where he lives with his wife Norma. Their love affair and family trials are a powerful thread through his remarkable book.

# IN
# THE PIT

## A CAPE BRETON
## COAL MINER

### RENNIE MACKENZIE

**Breton Books**
**Wreck Cove**

Editor: Ronald Caplan
Production Assistance: Bonnie Thompson
First Reader: Michelle Smith

Front Cover Photograph: Owen Fitzgerald
Back Cover, and on Pages 161-164: Photos by Leslie Shedden. Our thanks to Cyril MacDonald, Glace Bay, for his generous gift of the use of these photographs from his collection.

Our thanks, as well, to the Beaton Institute of Cape Breton Studies for Shedden photos: "Undercutting the Coal Seam" (C-57), "Automatic Door" (C-130), two photos of the shotfirer (C-62, C-63), "View into the Gob"—all in MG 14, 13, 8-E, Box 158.

"Man Carrying Chucks...at Lingan Mine, Eight East, July '83" photo by Owen Fitzgerald, Beaton Institute of Cape Breton Studies, Accession No. 83-6694-13994.

"Miners on the Rake at Donkin in 1925," the photo of a chuck block, and "View in the Wash House" courtesy the Miners' Museum, Glace Bay. Our thanks to Tom Miller and Alice Roberts for their help.

Thanks to Hugh Morrison, retired underground manager; to Hank Martin, retired manager; to fellow retired coal miners Bob Roper, Harry Corbett, Hughie MacDonald, and Art MacNeil. These old friends of the author salvaged many details. And thanks to Garth Robertson for his gracious efforts in reading this work. Any inaccuracies are the responsibility of the author.

Second Printing December 2001

The Canada Council | Le Conseil des Arts
for the Arts | du Canada

We acknowledge the support of
the Canada Council for the Arts for our publishing program.

We also acknowledge support from Cultural Affairs,
Nova Scotia Department of Tourism and Culture.

Tourism and Culture

### National Library of Canada Cataloguing in Publication Data

MacKenzie, Rennie, 1933-
  In the pit : a Cape Breton coal miner
  1st ed.
  ISBN 1-895415-70-5

    1. MacKenzie, Rennie, 1933-  2. Coal miners—Nova Scotia—
Biography.  3. Coal mines and mining—Nova Scotia—New Waterford.
I. Title.

TN806.C22N6 2001    622'.334'092    C2001-900556-3

# CONTENTS

THIS BOOK IS DEDICATED to my loving wife, Norma, and to our children, Noreen and Bruce, who encouraged its creation. Also to our grandchildren: Audrey, Brett, Allison, Tiffany, and Douglas.

It is also dedicated to all coal miners of the '50s and '60s who saw the brutal bull work they did as nothing out of the ordinary. Only they will know the "giants" killed in the course of a normal day, and the work they had to do just to get to work. Here's to those who remember shaker pans, dummy walls, chucks, and duffing shovels, and yes, to those who remember what a banjo is.

IN THE EARLY 1950s, the coal mining industry in Cape Breton began a move to mechanization, away from hand picks, pan shovels, and wooden chucks. Here is an account of one person's life as a coal miner before the change, and during its early stages.

The setting is 12 Colliery, New Waterford.

Dominion Number 12 Colliery, New Waterford—early view

# 1

# Graduation

I WAS A HIGH SCHOOL DROPOUT—a tragic dropout, because I came so close. I made it halfway
through Grade 11—in Central School in New Waterford. I could have made it all the way to graduation,
but who cared? Why should I bust my ass trying to
graduate? I didn't need this learning stuff to earn a
living. I had absolutely no desire to go to college, and
college was not a realistic option anyway.

My father told me many times: "Son, if you really
want to go to college, I will pay your way." But I did
not want to go to college, and my dad really did not en-
courage me along that line. It was all up to me. Deep
down, I knew my parents could not afford it.

Times were tough in Cape Breton in the '40s. The
necessities were always there, but higher academic
accomplishments were not part of serious family expectations. Both my grandfathers were coal miners,
and my father was a coal miner. Real expectations
were that I would be the same. That was the highest
expectation I had.

I blew my Grade 11 in the poolroom. Many a nice
day, stuck in class, I would hold up a sign on a scrib-
bler sheet to my best friend—behind me, one aisle to
the right—"Let's play hookey this afternoon." The an-

swer was always a gleeful "Yes" nod from him, and away we would go that afternoon on our bikes to the woods or, if we had any money, to the poolroom. The poolroom was more risky, since it was just about one block from the school.

As it turned out, we finally got caught in the poolroom. All hell broke loose for him, but I escaped because my parents lived, with no phone, about three miles away. They never found out, or if they did, did not want to deal with it because this teenage disobedience scared them. Or they were simply too busy making a living to be bothered.

My best friend's mother, however, did find out. She was a lower grade teacher at their school, so the binders really went on for him—a good thing, really, because he was disciplined into staying in school until he graduated. As for me, however—I dropped out, and looked at graduation much like a low class person would look at middle class, well-off people, celebrating something their expectations and efforts had brought about. This stuff never was part of my life and, as far as I could see, it never would be.

My father really wanted me to stay in school and make something of myself, but he could not handle a teenager's total disintegration and lack of interest in school. After the earlier man-to-man talk about the birds and the bees, parental resources were very limited. Authority could not motivate me to stay in school. My dad knew it. So the bottom line was: "Son, if you don't stay in school, get the hell out and work. Contribute something to this family I am trying to keep afloat."

I put my name in for the pit.

It only took a few months. While I was waiting, I

worked at a photography place developing films, then at Eaton's for the Christmas season. Then the call came—we had a phone now—to go to the main office of the company in Sydney to get examined for the pit.

The examination worried me. Could I pass it? I found out as much as I could about it—I wanted to be prepared. I heard that you had to fill out papers. That scared me. What questions would I have to answer? Guys said: "Don't worry! I made it, you sure as hell can." But I worried. I worried about the physical as well. Was I heavy enough? Did I have TB—I always had to go back for a second x ray when they were checking high school students. Also: the guys said the doctor squeezed your balls and asked you to cough. I wasn't sure if they were just trying to scare me or not, but I worried. Nobody had ever squeezed my balls before, and if they had, I sure as hell would not be trying to cough. I really wanted to practice this one to be sure I could do it, but no way! I wasn't asking anyone, not even one of my best friends, to squeeze my balls.

The day came. Dozens of guys were there at the same time as I was, and several doctors. It went well. I had worried for nothing. No question I could not answer, and for the physical, the doctor squeezed my balls so fast I hardly had time to cough, and it didn't hurt much at all.

Then the waiting. Did I pass everything—x rays and all? The doctor as much as told me: "No problem, you are healthy. I can tell." Still, I worried a bit. A week or so later I got the news: "Start day shift at 12 Colliery on Monday."

It was January 1951. I was eighteen.

**A view in the wash house.** Rennie MacKenzie: "You're looking at the benches where you sit down and change your clothes. Depending on what shift you're on—these are your pit clothes or your street clothes. And they stay up there while you're working. And after every shift, after every change, a guy comes along with a hose, and he hoses the benches and the floor—all the coal dust. Because pit clothes—they come down and you just whack them on the bench and knock the dust out of them, as much as you can—and then you put them on. And then this guy hoses it all down for the next shift.

"And you never wash your pit clothes. Not mine, anyway. Nobody ever took them home. You might take your socks, your underwear, that'd be it. You'd just wear out the pit clothes. Every vacation you took them home and washed them. A scattered time, maybe halfway through a year. You couldn't wash them home; you'd have to go to a laundromat to special washers. You usually threw them away. You just went to an Army Surplus and you got some more. Or any old rag at all, it didn't matter. They were just worn-out stuff that you didn't want any more, didn't care what happened to it. The only thing good there would be the boots and the helmet and the belt."

**Men on a rake heading into the mine around 1925.** Rennie said: "Well it's early, because there's no hardhats on those guys. But the rakes did not change that much. You've got there six seats. That'd be twelve men on each one of those rakes. And there'd be eight or nine rakes. You get a little over 100, 120 men on. Your two knees are up under your chin. The guy in front of you'd be leaning against your knees for support on his back. And guys sitting on the coupling."

MORE PHOTOGRAPHS ON PAGES 161 TO 164

# 2

# The Break-In Period

IT WAS 5:15 A.M. on a cold, frosty morning when I stepped out of the house on my way to the pit for my first shift. I had never seen the world like this before: cold, crisp and still. So this was part of my new life as a coal miner: early mornings. I was still a bit sleepy, but the beauty of the morning was alerting me to something special. I was captivated by the scene. My warm breath misted and lifted—like prayers of awe. It was just as dark as midnight, but it was different from midnight. Neither I nor the early winter morning felt like talking, so we came together as quiet companions.

There was a freshness that blessed me like it had been given a commission to do so. And the silence! It was not just quiet. It was a virgin silence, as if a cough or a loud noise would spoil something. The noise I heard seemed to belong quite well to the setting: the squeaky crunch of my boots as I walked on the frozen, pristine snow.

The sky also caught my attention. I didn't have to look up—the stars were busy looking down—making the scene even more beautiful, and commanding a deeper sense of awe.

In the midst of it all, I went philosophical. The thought crossed my mind that if I had to spend an hour here with no clothes on, this beauty would freeze me to death, and it would not know the difference! With that jab of reality, I turned left onto the road, and headed for the pit a mile and a half away.

There was a heavy iron weight on the end of a rope, the other end of which went through a pulley fastened to the top of the outside lamp house door. It needed oil badly. When I pulled to open the heavy hardwood door, the pulley squealed like a blackbird. I went in, walked down the long lamp house corridor and opened the inside door to the wash house. I no longer owned the morning. I had to share it now with about 200 murmuring men, all getting ready for day shift. As I went through the door, it felt like I had just passed the last rites of a secret lodge, and was allowed in. I grew up in the coal mining society, but only as a child and then as a student. This was the heart of that society. Now I was totally immersed in it. I was being baptized.

Tension and anxiety replaced the early morning peace. Once in the wash house, contrary to what I thought, a person did not simply "go to work." You had to find a "shift" first. Which meant that you had to ask an overman for that shift. I couldn't do that, because I was new. I had been told I would have to check in with the underground manager first. I asked around to find out who the underground manager was. It was J.P. Someone pointed out J.P. to me. J.P. was very busy! I waited my chance, then told him I was a new guy. "You will be working for Woody Longfellow," I was told, and the underground manager turned to the other guys who were wanting his attention. Then I put my pit clothes on, and picked up the lamp. It felt good strapping the battery onto the pit belt. This was big-league stuff.

Now to find Woody. I knew Woody—I had gone to school with two of his sons. But where in hell was he now? Tension was mounting. The last rake went down at 6:45. Finally, I spotted Woody, and told him the underground manager said I was working for him today. Woody said: "Yes, you go down with Nails," then walked away with not another clue.

A game was being played here, and I could recognize it. Sensitivity, care, and compassion had no part in this game—you were on your own! Those who were well established were saying: "Hey, look at me! I am important, and very busy." They knew a fresh guy just starting would be impressed. Egos needed stroking.

I was starting to sweat it out. Time was running short, and no one was about to take me by the hand and show me where to go. "Who in hell is Nails?" I asked one guy at random. "Dunno," was the reply and that guy kept going with whatever he had to do to get ready. After asking five or six guys, I got lucky. The next guy I asked about Nails said, "Oh, that's Henry Aspen. He gets the bus and goes down 14 Colliery." "Geeeezus—a bus! Where do you get this bus?" The tension went up a few more notches. "Oh, Pussycat runs it. It should be parked out there," and the guy pointed to the east side of the wash house. I went to where the guy pointed, and wouldn't you know—no bus! More tension.

I asked around again in semi-panic, and was told that Pussycat probably hadn't come back from his last trip to 14 Colliery. I went back out and waited, worrying that I might have missed the bus, but no. Coming towards the wash house was a small bus—a little guy with thick glasses at the wheel. When it stopped, another guy came from nowhere and got on the bus. I asked: "Are you Nails?" "That's what they say," was the reply, and with the relief of someone who had just awakened from a nightmare, I spilled my woes to Nails. No problem now. I was finally where I was supposed to be.

The bus started moving, and away we went to old 14 Colliery. I didn't know why—I was supposed to be working in 12 Colliery—but I went anyway. I was with Nails. That's all that mattered for now.

I found out during the bus ride that I would be working in the mined-out 15 East Level in 12 Colliery, but you could get there easier by going down 14 Colliery and walking through its old workings to the far end of 12 Colliery's 15 East Level. The two mines were connected underground. This was an option a lot of guys took when 15 East was in its last days, but still producing coal. Instead of walking underground, stooped over for a mile or two in 15 East Level, they took the bus over to 14 Colliery and walked underground for about half a mile, coming to their work from the other side.

In any event, the bus stopped close to 14 Colliery pithead. Nails and I walked the short distance to the man rake. This was a string of eight to ten wooden boxes with plank seats in them. The sides were about one and a half feet high. Each box could hold twelve men. The whole rake could transport about 120 men, but with 15 East finished, there were now only two: myself and Nails. Completely wrapped up in this new adventure, I got on the rake with Nails. I took some comfort in knowing that my father had worked in this pit, and had gone down the same rails as I was about to go down now for the very first time. Nails yanked four times on a small cable hanging from the roof of the slope. This "rapped" the rake down by ringing a bell at the hoist where there was a huge drum with about a mile of heavy steel rope wrapped around it. The hoist operator released the brake, and the steel rope started to unwind. The rake, which was on the end of the rope, started down.

It was still quite dark, and cold, but as we started down it got warmer, and the light from the lamps began to seem normal. No more sky and distance now. The roof and sides of the deep were swallowing us, and into this hole the rake went down, down, down. "How far do we go?" I shouted. "About a mile," Nails hollered back. The air smelled different—like the inside of some giant prehistoric beast. But soon, that too began to smell normal.

I was uneasy, but not really afraid—more excited than fearful about this new experience. This was another world—one I was seeing for the first time. A world of bent arch rails and huge timber supports that got too close for comfort as the rake passed under them. I nervously ducked about twice as far below the bent arch rails and cracked timber as was really needed. I was making very sure one did not clunk me on my hard hat. Nails sat nearly upright, barely tilting his head as he passed under the low rails. He was trying to impress me. I *was* impressed, but I was soon to be ticked off.

The rake stopped at an opening in the side of the deep. It was a level that led to where we would be working. It had a lower roof than the deep we were now on. Nails jumped off the rake and said: "Follow me." He then took off like the proverbial jack rabbit—still trying to be impressive. I followed, but I wasn't used to running half bent over, trying to hold my head straight so the lamp would shine where I was going. Nails knew that. He also knew that my legs would be like rubber very shortly, and they were. Not only that, but my lamp-weighted hard hat kept falling off. I had the lunch can in one hand, and while trying to hold my hard hat on with the other, did my damnedest to keep up to Nails. Just like in the wash house, care and compassion were definitely not a concern here. Right now, Nails was interested in fattening his ego at my expense.

Nails disappeared from that level and down a "cutoff"—a connecting passageway to another level. I got to where Nails turned, only to see his light disappear around another corner on the lower level. I knew there would be no use shouting for Nails to slow down—his ego would not hear. I cursed and gave it everything I had. Nails disappeared around another corner in the old workings, but I rushed to the spot and sighted Nails' light before it disappeared again.

Finally, Nails stopped and I caught up. We were at the spot where we would be working for this shift. We couldn't stand up because of the low roof—just as well, because my legs would not hold me up right now anyway. But I wouldn't tell that to Nails. I just thought to myself: "You @#!%& showoff!" and sat down next to him. Nails was trying to be impressive. He was soon to be deflated.

From out of nowhere a dim, reddish light appeared. It was a Davey safety lamp used by officials—a "glimmer." It was carried by Woody, the overman. He had gone down 12 Colliery much earlier, and walked the length of 15 East Level, arriving shortly after Nails and I to the place of work. The work consisted of salvaging used materials from the mined-out 15 East, and getting them out the old level so they could be used again in other parts of the pit. The used material in this case was a stretch of conveyor belt, about three feet wide and 100 feet or more long. In their last shift, the crew had all but rolled it up. Just a few feet more and it would be a drum of solid rubber belting weighing about 300 pounds. Woody, Nails, and I finished the job, then rolled it so the end was on the top.

At this point, nails were needed to fasten the loose end to the rest of the roll so the belting could be moved out without unrolling. Woody asked Nails for the nails. Nails looked at Woody with an "Oh, oh" look on his face, and said in a sinking voice: "I don't have any nails."

He should have had some nails, because he was told to bring some down. He had failed to do this one time not too long ago, and was blasted or sent up because he forgot them. I didn't have the whole story behind this, but apparently this was why Henry was called "Nails" in the first place, and the relatively short time since that incident explained why so few in the wash house knew who Nails was. He had been christened with that name for too short a time. Whatever, Woody let out a string of very uncomplimentary oaths, then bellowed: "YOU FORGOT!? Fill your coat—go up—you're FIRED!" Nails did not look a bit impressive now. Without a word, he filled his coat, picked up his lunch can, and left for the surface.

Now I was really impressed, not with Nails, but with overman Woody, and also a bit fearful of the man. "Geez," I thought, "could he fire me that quick?"

As green as I was, I sensed something unreal about what had just happened. Woody certainly had authority, but did he have the maturity to go with it? It seemed as if he had overplayed his hand with Nails—like he used this as an excuse to show his authority. He, too, wanted to be impressive—he wanted this new guy to know who was boss. Apparently this was close to the truth, since when Nails went to the manager, the manager immediately gave Nails his job back, and awarded him the shift he had lost when he was sent up.

In any event, after Woody sent Nails home, he told me to stay where I was—the rest of the crew would be there shortly. Then he left—his dim light vanishing like a ghost into the old workings. That left me alone. Here I was, scarcely an hour into my first shift in the coal mine, and I was totally and completely alone! To me it was like a labyrinth of tunnels, and I was in one of them. If the rest of the crew didn't show up, or went somewhere else, could I find my way back? That was not an option just now—I would do as Woody told me: stay here and wait.

Sitting in the silence beside the roll of belt, I took in my new surroundings. It was black—very black—and closed in. Everything was coal, and what was not coal was a clutter of dismantled mining equipment and timber. I quickly caught on to the fact that I had to shine my light on everything I wanted to see—each in its turn. I could not just look at something—I had to shine the light on it first, then look. As I shone my headlamp around, the walls of coal flashed reflections back to me. Light also sparkled from the bits of duff on the pavement—the floor—not unlike sun sparkling on a frosty, snow-covered field—black sparkle here instead of white, but it was still sparkle. Now I knew where they got the expression "black diamonds."

I really didn't mind being here alone. It was quiet—the same kind of quiet I had stepped into a few hours earlier. The world here was not so spacious and fresh, but it was the same world, and there was still peace in it. The peace now was accompanied by a sense of satisfaction. I had found my way through the wash house confusion and into my first shift. I had the sense of being "somebody" now.

In quiet times before, I had always worried about that. This place might be a black hole, but for now, it was my "place in the sun." My steel-toed boots, the pit belt with another belt on it for my battery, the lamp on my hard hat—it was the real coal miner's uniform, and it gave me an identity I was happy with. I felt good being here.

My budding bravado was interrupted by a slight noise to my right—along the high side rib. I shone my headlamp toward the sound. Geez!—the size of the rat! It stopped when the light shone on it—its tail longer than most rats I had seen. It was dirty, dark brown—and eerie, because its eyes, like the coal, shone my light back to me. I made a sudden jerk with my feet, and the rat scurried back into the darkness. How far back, I didn't know, but I wondered why it would try to pass by me in the first place. The lunch can! I shone the light on my lunch can—good! No eyes shining back at me from around the lunch can. Then I heard another, more welcome sound. I heard people talking, and saw the reflection of their lights. The rest of the crew were here. They had gone down 12 Colliery and walked in 15 East Level.

Cecil, Clayton, Spongy and Doc were their names,

but they didn't introduce themselves—no such formality in the pit. You simply waited until one guy called another by name, and remembered who answered to what name. I told them the story about Nails being fired, and to my relief they expressed openly—very openly—the suspicion I had. At least three oaths accompanied Woody's name each time they referred to him. Bottom line attitude was that Woody was not playing with a full deck. "Don't worry about him, b'y," they assured me. I felt very supported. I was thoroughly enjoying my new buddies.

This crew was known as the "construction" crew. It was not directly connected to production demands. That's why I was sent here. This crew was for new guys or guys with injuries or health problems. Nails, I learned, was a new guy, hired just a few weeks before me. Now he was sent somewhere else. The set-up was that working with this crew gave greenhorns a break-in period. The pace was slow—as a matter of fact, it was set by the crew itself. Woody was the boss, but he was not taken seriously by the crew even when he fired somebody. Nor was he taken seriously by management—which was probably why he fired somebody—he was pissed off because he wasn't taken seriously! Woody would say: "I want ten pans dismantled today, and ready to go out."

But that was unrealistic. The guys would listen to Woody's rantings, then survey the situation and decide: "We'll get four pans out today"—which was realistic, because these things just did not dismantle automatically and pile themselves on a tram. They weren't worried about satisfying Woody, but they did worry about satisfying management. Sooner or later the manager would find out how they were doing, and it had better be adequate! It was pans on the Sydney Mines Loader that we were dismantling.

Since this is what we would be doing, I was very interested in the pans. They were big, and looked heavy. Moving them around was not going to be a picnic. They were made of steel about the thickness and size of a 4-by-8 sheet of gyprock. They had a four-inch skirt down the sides, but not on the ends. On top, they had three or four sets of rollers crossways on the pan, upon which a conveyor belt ran. Each set of rollers consisted of a horizontal middle roller, and two smaller rollers tilted upwards at both ends of this middle roller. This arrangement lifted the sides of the rubber conveyor belt as it was drawn over the rollers, so the coal would not fall off the edge of the belt.

On the bottom of the pans were two or three rollers that went straight across the pan. These were for the empty belt that returned underneath the pans. Also on the underside of the pans were wheels. Ten or twelve of these pans were joined together in a line and set on rails. As the coal was taken off the wall, this whole conveyor assembly was moved inward to fresh coal. Fifteen East, however, was done. No more coal here now. That's why the construction crew had to dismantle this assembly and get these pans and conveyor belt to other locations where they could be used again.

Close to the end of the shift, I saw firsthand that four pans was an honest, realistic goal, simply because ninety-nine percent of the bolts holding the pans together, and the wheels and rollers on them, were rusted and seized solid. Forget the luxury of twisting the nuts off the bolts—they had to be cut off with hammer and chisel, or hacksaw. Complicating the process was the fact that there was seldom enough room to swing a hammer, or even to work a hacksaw. It was quite a job just to get at the bolts. This was an old level, which meant that it was after closing in until the roof, in places, was barely a few inches above the conveyor belt and pans. Even in newer levels, if an oversized lump of coal came on this belt, it would jam to the roof and stop the loader. There was never much room over these things. There was less in this older 15 East Level. Yes, four pans a shift were plenty.

It was 1:45 P.M. and this part of the shift was over. This was a bit early, but the guys were going back the way they came in—through 15 East Level—and it was a long walk. One and one half miles was no exaggeration. I was going with them. Going back through 14 Colliery to the bus was not an option for me now, since Nails was not there to "guide" me back through the old workings. Besides, I did not want to leave the company of my new buddies. We had bonded well—so well that the shift with these guys had not really seemed like work—it was more like fun.

Now my first shift was over, and with a "Let's go, b'ys," from Cecil, everyone picked up their lunch cans and started out, crawling the first few hundred feet past the machinery, then starting in for a long, mostly bent over, walk.

I could see why the guys pressed for production would choose to take the bus to 14 Colliery. The walk in or out of 15 East took a lot of energy—energy that could be better used doing whatever they had to do to get the coal out. I and my buddies were not pressed, so we walked. Finally, we came to the landing—the outside end of the level. I was about to be introduced to a new adventure—a far cry from a quiet bus ride.

It was just Nails and I who had gone down on the

rake in 14 Colliery. I didn't realize it then, but that was a real luxury—just two of us on the whole rake. No such luxuries here—this was 12 Colliery. My buddies and I now walked across an auxiliary deep for hauling coal. "Auxiliary" meaning it was the second of two almost-in-line, mile-long deeps.

The main deep stopped a mile or so down. Then there was another hoist and another deep: the auxiliary deep which went another mile down. After crossing this deep, and walking a short way in the west level on the other side of it, we came to another deep parallel to the one we had just crossed. This one was the auxiliary back deep—"back" meaning the deep for hauling men only. This back deep is where the rake was. One or two men no doubt travelled on this rake during the shift for work-related reasons, but at the end of the shift—no such tranquility—look out!

The rake would hold 120 men—legally—that is, with no one riding the couplings between the individual sections of the rake. The problem was: there were a lot more than 120 men waiting to go up! This meant that you had to be quick. As the rake arrived, if you saw a place to sit, get it fast because, before the rake stopped or even slowed down, guys were jumping on it—not only on the seats, but also on the couplings when all the seats were taken. The couplings could hold four men, but no one was supposed to ride the couplings. Technically, management could fire anyone caught riding the couplings, but management itself rode the couplings, so they turned a blind eye.

It was another matter, however, if some adventurous, hurried soul stepped on to a full trip of coal as it started up the other deep—the one my buddies and I had just crossed over. Management turned no blind eye to this. If you were caught on a full trip by top management, it was automatic—you were fired. More than one unfortunate full trip rider was decapitated when, for some unknown reason, he stuck his head above the wildly speeding boxes and into the roof.

In any event, the adventure into which I was to be introduced started with the fact that this much over-loaded rake, couplings and all, that I was now on—and on the way up—was in the auxiliary back deep. This meant that, after travelling so far, everyone on this rake had to get off, and get on another rake in the main back deep—the one that would take us to the surface. As I would later find out, sitting on a coupling as one of four men was *very* uncomfortable.

You had to keep shifting position so that the edge of the two-inch plank you were sitting on would not stop blood flow to your legs. With every bad rail joint the rake went over, the edge of the plank jolted in deeper—reaching for bone. Everyone knew this. They also knew that there were thirty or forty men on the couplings of this rake who were vowing that they would have a good seat on the rake going to the surface. Complicating matters was the fact that there would be half a dozen or so men already on the main back deep rake. Bottom line was: there were more men on this rake than there were seats for them on the next rake to the surface.

So, as soon as this rake slowed down to a slower speed than a man could run uphill, everyone started to bail off, and run like hell up to the top of the deep and into a horizontal "transfer" passage that con-nected to the main back deep. This was the part I did not know about. Once I stepped off the rake, whether I wanted it or not, I was in one hell of a mad rush, and there was just no room to get out of the way, or go around anyone. I had to join the stampede. Gawd help any guy who fell down. He would surely wear the bruises from dozens of pit boots that had absolutely nowhere to go except over his prostrate body.

Once 150 men got running in a line in a narrow tunnel, stopping was definitely not an option, especially up front. Since I was about in the middle of the stampede, I did okay. I managed to get a good seat on the final rake to the surface. With a twinge of guilt I watched older or disabled guys walking in vain up and down the length of the loaded rake looking for a place to get on. Finding none, they crawled into a "waiting head" and waited for the next rake that would get them to the surface—half an hour later than the quick and nimble.

Once up, it was more of the same, except now it was not rake to rake, but rake to showers. It was the same scene, with improvements. The guys still bailed off the rake before it stopped, but on the surface now there was room to spread out, so the faster guys went around the slower ones and into the wash house, shouting their check numbers as they unfastened their batteries and laid them on the long lamp house countertop. Most of them didn't even have to shout their number—the checker knew it from memory, and tossed it on the countertop as soon as the guy appeared. Eight to ten check numbers were always on the counter at once—just pick up your own and go.

The dry pulley that squealed like a blackbird never got the chance for a full squeal now—it just squeaked as the door closed only a few inches before being jerked open again by the next guy.

I unstrapped my battery, laid it on the counter,

and shouted: "1033!" The checker tossed an oval-shaped, silver-dollar-sized piece of brass on the counter. It had 1033 stamped in it. I picked it up, stuck it in my pit helmet where the lamp used to be, and continued on to my hook. The hook was something like a pulley clothesline, only vertical and shorter. It was fastened on the top end to the wash house roof rafters about fifteen or twenty feet up. The bottom end was hooked onto a horizontal bar that was part of a long, low, backless bench used by ten or more men to sit or stand on while changing clothes. I lifted the hook off the bar and lowered my street clothes down from the rafters.

Now I had the same apprehension I had in the morning when it came time to take my clothes off. I didn't like stripping naked in a crowd—even if all were men. I had never done this before. Not only that, I had never taken a shower with anyone before. That was about to change. Ten or fifteen assorted bare arses were already invading the showers. It was obvious that no one was in the least bit concerned with themselves or anyone else being naked. The concern was to get in the showers while there was still room.

I stripped and joined the moon river, but too late. There were three, sometimes four and five men to each shower. Much too crowded. So, like a few other naked souls, I went back to my hook. I hung around in my birthday suit and waited.

Not only did the miners not care about being naked in a crowd. They made fun of each other's usually secret parts. If a guy had an exceptionally small "handle," he was kidded about it. Like: "Hey Joe, what's the good of that thing? All it can do to a woman is tickle the outside and drive the inside crazy." All

Joe could do was grin and bear it with a "Suck me arse." That switched on hoots of laughter from all who heard. Joe had no choice but to get used to it! Either that, or go home full of coal dust, and wash at home.

On the other hand, some guys were exceptionally well hung. One such guy always got a response when he stripped off, especially if it was Friday, and all were in a good mood. "Hey Sammy," someone would yell, "how about a lend of that thing for the weekend." "No," Sammy would reply, "just let me know when your wife is home alone." Again to Sammy: "Hey Sammy, did you eat an elephant?" "No," Sammy says, "why?" "His trunk is hanging out," came the reply. More hoots of laughter.

When the bare bodies thinned out a bit, I tried again. There were still enough men there that I had to shower with someone else—but down to two or three guys to a shower. When the other guys moved out, I got wet, then moved out again and started scrubbing. I had just started scrubbing when another guy handed me soap and turned his back to me. For an instant, I was puzzled, but the guy saw the greenhorn look on my face, and said: "Wash my back." I did, then the guy washed my back. Perfect strangers—yet here we were, showering together and washing each other! I took it all in stride.

THE NEXT SHIFT turned out to be a bit easier, but it had a surprise. We had to walk just as far, but were not to work in 15 East Level this day. We had to get some materials out of a cutoff that joined the inside of 15 East at a 90-degree angle. The cutoff was much more spacious, so we easily dismantled more material than expected. Then we made the always happy deci-

sion: "Let's eat, b'ys!" No argument with that—
besides, it was time for lunch. I was at the high side of
my buddies. Doc, Spongy, Clayton and Cecil were all
in a descending line towards the level below. All
opened our lunch cans and were enjoying sandwiches
and chatter. For me, this was the very best time of
the shift.

But then it happened! Cecil was the bottommost
diner today. In the midst of munching and stories, Cecil let out a roar of curses as if someone had just
slapped him in the face. He threw his sandwich in his
can, and slammed the can shut. A split second later,
Clayton did the same—then Spongy, then Doc. I was
alarmed and ready to run, but only for a second. I
quickly became aware of why the guys were cursing so
violently.

For whatever reason, another guy, Angus—
whom they all knew—had been sent in with a message. Angus, however, did not deliver the message
right away. Once he saw his buddies up the cutoff, he
turned out his light so he would not be seen, and delivered his daily bowel movement at the bottom of the
cutoff. The ventilating air, which went up the cutoff,
did the rest. It was a perfect coal mine "gotcha."

When Angus came up the cutoff, the most visible
part of him was his teeth. He was greeted with a four-
mouth volley of curses. "What's the matter, b'ys?" he
asked with a huge grin. "You know what's wrong, you
!@#$%^&* bastard!"—and they continued to bury him
in curses, describing his guts as the sickest, most dis-
eased dead flesh imaginable. "You didn't eat that, you
&%*$#@—it crawled up your hole and died." The more
the curses, the more Angus's teeth flashed. He was
loving it. He knew he'd got us good. We knew it too.

## The Break-In Period

NOT ALL THE SHIFTS I had with the construction crew were this easy and eventful, but all were enjoyable. Even the ones working on the pans on the main, very squeezed-in level. The hardest part here was getting at the nuts and bolts on the low side—the side farthest from the surface—because the pans were close against this side. There was more room on the high side, since there was a haulage road there. The bolts here yielded easily to the brutal attacks with the hammer and chisel, but the low side bolts were sometimes next to impossible. Just to get to them meant one guy lying on his side and reaching with one hand to the bolt he couldn't see. Then, by feel only, get a stilson wrench on it and lock it so another guy could beat it, chisel it, saw it and curse it from underneath the pan.

Once disconnected, it was another matter to get the pan out. There was no room to stand it on edge and, most of the time, no room to leave it flat and carry it out the old haulage road. More likely, it had to be held at a 45-degree angle and pushed and pulled, inches at a time, until an open spot in the tunnel was reached. The men on the in side of the pan had to stay there until the pan was out. There was no way to get around it.

The pace was slow but the work was hard. There was no easy way. Some pans came easier than others but all were hard going.

ONE DAY WOODY TOOK ME on a tour of a working part of the mine. This was really a signal that my days in 15 East with the construction crew were coming to an end. Woody took me in 16 East Level, which was at the top of 17 East Wall—a wall in full production. The smell in this level was very different. I could almost taste new coal, and I *could* taste the smoke that came from the blasting powder. This was a very busy place. Woody took me to a hole in the low side of the level where all the smoke and dust was coming from. It was called a "gundy" hole, and it was just big enough for a man to crawl through. It was like a pit within a pit. I could hear machinery going and men shouting to one another.

But I was not at all attracted to the idea of crawling through that hole to where the action was. I was later to find out that the wind in that hole was very close to hurricane force. Thankfully, Woody did not go there. He suggested it was too busy and dangerous for a greenhorn, but I sensed that Woody was not a bit fussy about going through that hole either. He explained what he could, then continued on in 16 East Level.

The gundy hole was for ventilation of 17 East, and where timber and other materials were carried to the top of the wall and sent down. It was much easier sending stuff down the operating pan line than pushing it up the wall.

Once in past the top of the wall, it was much like 15 East—quiet, peaceful, and closing in. There was nothing going on in here now, but Woody kept travelling anyway. He was heading for a "donkey" farther in. A donkey was a smaller version of the hoist that let men down the pit and hauled coal out. It had the usual drum with steel rope wound on it, but it was a smaller drum and smaller rope. On the end of this rope was a trip—a string of about fifteen steel boxes all linked together—just like open railway cars, but much smaller. This donkey haulage supplied 17 East with materials, and took out stone from where the level was "brushed"—that is, made higher and wider where it had started to close in.

The boxes were loaded with stone—heavier than coal—much heavier. Woody knew this loaded trip was ready to go out. This meant that if he and I got on it, we would be spared the walk back out. A drive out was always a luxury in the coal mine. Woody spoke to the donkey runner and told him he and I would be on the trip, and asked him to take it easy. Yeah, sure! If ever there was a request made in vain, that was it.

Woody and I got in the innermost box on top of the stone. We were still well below the top of the box since, because of its weight, each box was only half filled with stone. The donkey runner let the brake off—and the son of a bitch never put it back on until the trip was ready to pile up on the landing at the outside end of the level!

It started slow, and I thought: "This is great—a ride out." It was a ride all right! When the strain came on the couplings, I felt the boxes pull apart and speed up as the front ones started down a grade. Then the back ones bumped up, and pushed the trip faster. This was quite fast enough, I thought, but it was not to be. The boxes pulled apart again and again, each time going faster as the front ones went down grade after grade. By now, the roof—which was all I could see—was a blur, and the roar of steel wheels rolling on steel rails was all I could hear.

Just when the trip was going as fast as I thought it could go, the front boxes yanked apart again and doubled in speed, only to be pushed by the weight of the back boxes when they got to the same downward grade. I felt like I was on a falling rock. I lifted my head a bit and shouted to Woody: "The rope must have

25

come off!" Woody's voice was in a pitch between a roar and a scream: "Keep your head down!" Good advice, because had any part of my body touched the roof, it would have stayed right there, and the rest of me would have kept going.

Finally, I felt a yank on the box we were in. That crazy, sadistic, shit-headed dingbat on the donkey finally applied the brake—not because he wanted to, but because he had to. The trip was approaching the landing at the end of the level, and had to be stopped. There were two sets of tracks here—one for the full trip, and one for the empty trip that came in from the deep. If the full trip were not slowed down, it surely would have jumped the road when it switched from the straight level to the high side full road. But slowed down now to a sensible speed, the boxes smoothly switched to the high road, came to where they should be, and stopped.

Woody and I got out of the box, and I wonder to this day why Woody, always so ready to explode, simply mumbled under his breath about the donkey runner. However, I thought I could detect "bastard" at the end of his mumbling.

That shift was over and we headed for the back deep rake and the surface. No longer a pure greenhorn, I was better prepared now for the end-of-the-shift stampede. It didn't take long to catch on. As I suspected, my break-in time was about to come to an end. The next day, the underground manager came to me and said: "You will be working for Sput Turner today in 18 West." The party was over.

# 3

# 18 West

EIGHTEEN WEST was the second worst wall in the pit—not because of the geology of the place, but because of the velocity of the ventilating air. It approached gundy hole proportions. I never really knew why, but I guessed it was something like the holes in a flute. If all holes were open, you would have to blow like hell to get air to the bottom hole, because a lot would escape out of the top holes. Seventeen and 18 West were the top walls, and air had to get down to 21 West, the bottom "hole." Whatever—I had heard of 18 West, and of Sput, the overman. Neither were of good report.

I was to go down as a pan shifter on Number One pan line. There were three pan lines—one big line, really, with twenty or thirty pans allotted to each of three engines. The pan line moved the coal along from where it was loaded. Each pan was about seven feet long and three feet wide, made of half-inch steel plate. Each one weighed 200 pounds. Imagine an ordinary bread pan seven feet long and three feet wide, pushed out at the sides and open at the ends. That gives a general idea, except that the sides of the pans had a step fold in them for strength.

These pans were bolted to one another at their bottom corners by four big, one-inch-diameter, Jshaped bolts. They were much like an ordinary bolt, except that instead of a nut-shaped head, the bolt was doubled back at the head end into a J shape. The bend stopped the bolt from pulling through the hole. The bolts passed through the corner holes on the outsides of the pans, joining them together, and a big nut was screwed on each threaded end. The devil himself could not get these pans apart once they were securely bolted at all corners.

On this particular Number One pan line, twenty-one pans were bolted together. They were called shaker pans because they were pulled up hill by a compressed-air, single-piston engine for about one and a half feet—then pushed down and quickly jerked back up. The coal on them was shaken down the pan line to a conveyor belt at the bottom of the wall. Every second day—every two shifts of loading coal—this whole pan line, engine and all, had to be dismantled, and then reassembled over against the wall face again. This was a maintenance shift. If this was your job, you were a pan shifter. It was as a pan shifter that I was to get a taste of what it was really like to be a coal miner.

This machinery was big and heavy, but the weight and size of it were not really the problem. A crew of three miners, in good shape, could do the job. The problem was that there was no room to get at this brutal stuff. The pans themselves were almost buried in the coal that spilled off during the two shifts that the loaders shoveled coal on them. Between where the pans were and the coal face where they had to be shifted, there were two-and-a-half by two-and-a-half foot "chucks"—supporting pillars built from pavement to roof about every five feet. These wood-block chucks could not be moved. There were also quite a few supporting timber the loaders had put up where the coal they loaded used to be. Some of these could be temporarily removed.

On the other side of the pans—the gob side—were more chucks, worse spillage, and a two-inch, steel-pipe air line that rested up against the bolts. Compounding the whole cluttered mess was the fact that the roof was no more than five and a half feet from the pavement (bottom), and one good foot of that space was taken up by "duff." Duff was the granular coal ripped out from under the full length of the coal wall by a Samson cutting machine, leaving a four-inch space under the coal so it could be blasted down. Add to this the worst characteristic of 18 West: the unrelenting force of the dust- and smoke-filled ventilating air that stung the eyes and kept them watering and irritated for the full shift. Once on the surface, the guys who worked in 18 West could be picked out because of their reddened eyes. It was no picnic!

My first shift here was long and hard. There was no regular, well-established pan shifting crew. As soon as a guy could get the hell out of this place, he left. So I started my first shift as a pan shifter, working with two men who were seasoned miners, but who were new to this place in 18 West. The head pan shifter, Bruno, was not the least bit happy that he had to tackle a job like this with a greenhorn. He lamented that he had to carry this new guy around on his shovel all day—meaning me. As for the guy on the bolts, he just didn't give a damn. If he couldn't get at a bolt, he stopped trying and waited for the disgruntled Bruno and I to catch up. Then the three of us had to work on that bolt.

By the time we got to the engine, every one of my

muscles were screaming and my eyes were burning out of my head from that damned "wind." My knees were almost raw from working on them, and my back was scraped and bleeding from the times I forgot where I was and tried to stand up. As if that were not bad enough, my light was going dim. In the face of this, the engine still had to be shifted and set up, and three more pans after that. It was a long, hard shift. By the time we finished, the loaders were walking up the wall to start the production shift. I barely had the strength to crawl down the wall and go home. If this was to be my regular day, I wondered how long I could keep it up.

It got even worse! Not the next pan shifting day, since that was in 20 West, as it was every second day. And 20 West was a warmer level, with no wind and a pleasant overman. Still not a regular pan crew, but we finished on time that day.

Then it was back to 18 West again. This was my third shift on the pans. It was the worst shift I ever had in the coal mine.

Being a new guy, I was the only pan shifter who showed up for Number One pan line. There was no one for head pan shifter or bolt boy. The seasoned guys knew better than to come down for a shift here. Sput, the overman, was in a bad mood, as usual. He asked me where the spanners were for the bolts. I wasn't on the bolts the last shift here, so I didn't know. My guess was that the guy who was on the bolts didn't give a damn where he left them—lucky now if anybody ever found them.

Sput cursed me, right to my face. He told me I was a useless arsehole, good for nothing. He then spit, and walked away.

I was devastated. I crawled just a few feet up the

wall by myself. I was kneeling in the duff with my hard hat touching the roof. The black sparkle from the duff and coal face flashed at me again, but there was no quiet peace now like on my first shift in 15 East. Nobody had ever cursed me like that before. I looked at the pans impossibly buried in spillage, thought of the whole pan line and engine, and was overwhelmed by the size of the task that seemed to be on my shoulders. Worse, I was completely demoralized by the cursing I got from the overman.

Tears came to my eyes, but not from the ventilating air. I was starting to cry. Desperately I longed for my father to be by my side now, saying something like: "Don't worry about this stuff, son. Here, grab that pan and let's go." But I was alone. I had to make my own way through this one. I wanted to quit and go home, but what would I ever tell my father? Or anyone else for that matter. I had to work this one through.

Soon, two guys came up the wall, one with a set of spanners. One of them said, "You go on the bolts. Me and Bonnie here will shift the pans." Both of them were loaders—seasoned into the hardest work in the pit. This was not a piece of cake for them, but it was no threat; and they gave me what I so desperately needed—words of encouragement and assurance. "We'll make 'er, b'y, just hang in there." "Make 'er" we did—late, for sure, but the job that looked so impossible to me got done, and I helped do it.

I was never the same after that shift. I felt fully "broke in" now. I was hardened physically a little bit more, but emotionally, I was hardened a whole lot more. I actually wanted Sput to curse me again, so I could tell him to go screw himself, and supply him with a good description of just what this new guy thought of him. The loaders not only shifted the pans, they also shifted my emotional attitude. These guys were real men—heroes to me. I wanted to be like them.

As it turned out, I was to see Sput in a situation almost completely reversed: the pan crew cursing Sput, and Sput melting under the onslaught. This was the pan crew formed in the next few days. The lamenting Bruno was replaced by Fred. Good riddance, as far as I was concerned. Sparky also came on board as bolt boy. Now it was Fred, Sparky and I. Fred was head pan shifter, and as far as I could see, completely unflappable. He took anything and everything in stride. Sput, the overman, was not going to pressure this guy. Sparky was also a very seasoned miner. He was an older man—small build, no teeth, and a raspy voice. Sparky had a unique talent: whenever he started cursing, it was nice to hear—like a song. On Friday, when everyone was in a good mood, the guys on the wall would greet Sparky with any derogatory term they could think of just to get him going. Everyone close enough would listen with pleasure as raspy-voiced Sparky, in jest, would tell someone who they were, where they could go, and what they could do. It was fun to be dressed down by Sparky.

Our pan shifting crew worked well together, but we were still new to 18 West, Number One pan line, so Sput kept right on us. He wanted to be sure the pan line was finished in time for the coal shift. His pushy anxiety was soon to backfire.

This day, things were late in 18 West, as usual, and Sput was worried, as usual. He watched every move. He came to nose in when the engine was being timbered—jammed to the roof with six timber to keep it from moving—and he stayed. When the pans were going on over the engine, and being connected to Number Two pan line, he crawled to the air valve for Number One engine and waited there.

When all the pans were connected, Sput was over eager to open the valve and try the engine to see if it was secure. He should have left that to Fred. The valve had only a four-inch handle on it—too short for good control. He should have had a two-foot-long piece of pipe on it as an extension, because the short handle would stick when the valve was partly open, then when it was pushed harder would, without warning, open fully. That is exactly what this one did on Sput.

When it first opened, it didn't let enough air to the engine to make it go, so Sput pushed harder. The valve cleared itself, and went to wide open position accidentally. Full pressure—at least 100 pounds per square inch—went to the freshly timbered engine. The thing literally leapt to life. It was not supposed to move even an inch, but now it was slightly airborne, timber flying off it in all directions, and banging like hell.

In about three seconds the thing just sat there hissing air. It now had to be repositioned and re-timbered. My heart sank, but not Sparky's! Never before did I hear someone cursing like Sparky was now cursing Sput—and not in jest!—*and* not just a few choice words, but "up one side and down the other" as the saying goes. He cursed Sput a thousand times more than Sput had cursed me a week or so earlier.

Sput could have fired Sparky on the spot, but he was "over a barrel." This pan line had to be ready for the coal shift, or Sput would have to answer tough questions from management. Questions made even tougher because he was the one who screwed up. All his authority drained from him, and he turned into a stuttering idiot. In between curses, Sparky threatened to leave for home immediately—which he could have done legally, since his eight hours were up. When Sput heard this he disintegrated. He literally started to whine, beg and plead with the crew to stay down and set up the engine again. Fred calmly agreed. After being told by Sparky to piss off several times, Sput did just that. Sparky and I hung in with Fred and set the engine up again. It was late when we finished. When we finally started down the wall for home, we met the fresh-faced bright-lighted loaders on the way up to their sections for the production shift.

EVERY DAY ON 18 WEST was a bad one, but the pan shifting crew was a good one. My buddies and I bonded well together, but it was a different kind of bonding than with the construction crew. Things were more serious on a producing wall, and the stakes were higher. There was no goal-setting option here—like the four pans a day in 15 East. The goal here was to finish the job no matter how hard it was. Consequently, the comradeship was more like soldiers in a battle than members on a hockey team. This crew depended more upon one another.

My part in the crew was as helper to Fred, the head pan shifter. Sparky was on the bolts. He would go up the whole pan line, taking out all the bolts he could. Then he would come back down and start to tighten the bolts on the shifted pans. Once or twice he would have to leave a bolt in the not-yet-shifted pans until Fred and I got to it. Then the three of us would move the bolt-connected pans as a unit, so Sparky could get at the bolt.

Once the bolts were out of the very first, bottom-most pan, however, shifting began in earnest. Fred would look at it and decide the best way to move it around the chucks and timber to the wall face. Each pan had to be planned, much like furniture movers would decide how to best move a chesterfield from a truck and through to the room where it was supposed to go. Once Fred decided, he told me. Then we both knew the route to take—which meant a lot. These things were heavy. Once Fred and I worked a few shifts together, we knew when and how each other would move. Soon, one word was enough. It was both a command and a directive: "left," "right," "up," and so on. It made things much easier.

The shifting began with Fred shoveling about a three-foot-square clearing in the duff by the wall face. Then we would go to the pan to be shifted, and move it off the "cradle" it was resting on. This cradle was a two-foot-square steel frame, the sides of which were indented to cradle a set of wheels. These wheels were solid steel about eight inches in diameter and joined with a one-inch diameter steel axle. This "set" of wheels moved as a solid unit. I dug the cradle out of the spillage using a small miner's pick. I stuck one end of the pick under the cradle frame and pulled on the pick handle to pry the cradle up. I broke more than one pick handle doing this. Once freed from the spil-lage, I tossed it to the coal face along with the wheels and two chuck blocks upon which the cradle was set.

Fred took this assembly and set it up again at the coal face in the spot he had cleared for it. Then I went to the gob side of the pan, usually on my knees, with

Fred on the face side. With fingers under the top lip of the pan, we heaved in unison, lifting and pulling the pan a foot or so at a time, around chucks and between timber. More than once, the thing would get stuck, and we would have to draw a timber, or try another route.

Once at the face, we set it back on its wheels, cradle and blocks, and I bolted it to the last pan we had shifted. A matching cradle was welded to the bottom of each pan so that the whole pan line moved up and down on the wheels. There were about twenty-one sets of wheels—a set for each pan. Fred and I were now ready for the next pan to go above and in line with this one, and so on.

This operation had to be repeated once for each pan, most often in severely cramped quarters. It was not unusual for me to be lying on my side in order to lift the gob side of the pan. It used to make me grin when I would remember being told, and even shown posters, how to lift correctly. "Feet planted solidly, knees bent, back straight...." Yeah, sure. How about: "With your back against the roof, one foot set flatly in the west, knee under chin, the other leg straight and a few feet southeast with a steel pan scraping your shin...." There, b'y, lift now!

If we had the room to get a good lift on the pan, and room to heave it, Fred and I could heave a pan the seven-foot length of itself. But there was never the room. Sometimes we could only move a pan inches at a time. After we worked our way up the pan line for about eighteen pans, it was drive-pan-and-engine moving time. The ordinary pans were bad enough, but from here on, the work got more brutal. However, it was time out for lunch at this point.

There was no set lunchtime in the pit. When a guy was hungry, and saw the chance, he ate. A lot of guys set their own time. For example: "We'll eat after we draw the back line of chucks," or, in the case of the pan shifting crew: "We'll eat when we get to the engine." There was no such thing as the whole pit, or even this wall, stopping for lunch.

In this case, as in many another time, it would have been nice to have the whole wall shut down for lunch, because no sooner did my buddies and I sit down and open our lunch cans, when we heard: "tink, tink, tink, tink..." twenty or thirty times. It was the pipefitter who came just behind Fred and me. He was shifting the two-inch steel pipe that delivered compressed air to the pan engines, jackhammers, etc. He, too, had it shifted now up to the pan engine, and was ready to blow all the bits and pieces of coal out of it.

He was down the wall on the level below at the live air valve—too far away to shout a warning. Even if he did shout, it would be passed off as just another shout. So he beat on the pipeline with his pipe wrench. That was the signal that he was about to blow out the line, and this "tinking" could be heard very clearly all along the pipeline. When we heard this, we stopped eating and closed our lunch cans. In a minute, it was going to get very, very dusty. "Tink, tink, tink, tink...." one more time. If the pipefitter happened to be a bit over cautious and kept lunchers waiting while he "tinked" again, someone—probably Sparky—would surely say: "Blow the gawd-damned thing out, willya!" even though they knew the pipefitter couldn't hear the frustrated request.

This time, however, after two warnings, there was a low "whooshing" sound from the end of the open pipe—enough for a final alert to anyone near the open-ended pipe to get the hell out of the way. Bits of coal were about to fly like bullets. The pipefitter then opened the valve all the way. The roar was deafening, the dust was blinding and the coal in front of the pipe was in command. It made everyone turn their backs to it, and even then, if hit by some, it would really sting. It seemed like a longer time, but it was only about fifteen seconds. Everyone accepted it as a necessary evil. When the dust cleared, which didn't take long in the 18 West wind, cans opened again and lunch continued. As always, lunchtime with the guys was the best part of the shift for me.

A favourite lunchtime conversation would be hunting and fishing. In replying to a fishing story once, one guy said: "Every time we go fishing, some stupid *!#@ wants to fish"—meaning they had enough booze along for a prolonged drinking party, and he wanted to drink instead of fish. Favourite spots would be discussed, and how to get there. It was not uncommon for several miners to know the same spot, and add tidbits of information about it, like: "There is a fresh chopping there now. I've seen deer there." Very often, this conversation would blossom into deeper and more lasting friendships, because the guy who was describing an interesting spot would invite others to come with him on Saturday. I went on several rabbit-hunting trips just from these lunchtime conversations—trips with guys who owned beagles—rabbit-hunting hounds.

Inevitably, the talk would turn to women—naked women, with vivid descriptions of various parts of the female anatomy, much to the pleasure of all who listened. Never would a miner say his girl friend's name.

If it were found out, she would be the object of jokes all day. Someone would hold up a pick horizontally and say: "Look at that, that's the width of the arse on Mabel." Someone would always say they had someone else's girl friend on a date first, and "describe" a birth mark or a mole she had on part of her body that no boy was supposed to be able to see. It was all in fun, and lightened up the day. Sometimes it lengthened the lunchtime. One underground manager loved to hear the guys describing what they did with women. If he happened to be there when the guys were having their lunch, he would not mention getting back to work—as long as the stories held his interest.

DURING LUNCH Fred, especially, would be checking out the engine and surroundings, and planning ahead. Once lunch was over, and a fresh bite of MacDonald's Twist chewing tobacco tucked in the jaw, we continued our assault on the remainder of the pan line. The drive pan was next. The work was second only to the engine in brutality. It weighed about three times as much as an ordinary pan, and was always directly behind a chuck. This meant it had to be moved the length of itself down or up the wall, over to the face, then down or up again depending upon which way it was moved in the first place. This route was bad enough with an ordinary pan, but it was pure brute bullwork to move the drive pan this way. All three of us were needed for this pan. After sweat, grunts, heaves and curses, the drive pan was persuaded into position.

No let-up in the bullwork! Now the engine. This was the number one brute—a thousand-pound iron and steel behemoth. It was roughly cylindrical in shape—about four feet long and one and a half feet in diameter. It was solidly set in a frame of six-inch steel I-beams, the frame being about five feet square. There was a polished steel piston rod sticking out the front of the engine—three to four feet long and two inches in diameter—with a huge yoke on it. This rod and yoke would be the same shape as a tuning fork sawed off short at the fork end, but hundreds of times larger. This piston rod was connected to the drive pan.

All this would be just in a day's work if it weren't for the fact that this engine brute was completely buried in impacted spillage. I looked at it and wondered again: "How in hell will we ever get that thing to the coal face?" The answer was to be the same every time: "Brute bullwork!" Adding to the misery was the fact that there were six timber bracing the engine that had to be knocked down. More likely than not, some of the roof would come down with them.

Some of the roof did come in, but really not that much this time. I started. It was my job to "find" this engine. I was learning to take it easy—not to tear my guts out at this stuff. I took an easygoing shovelful at a time, and soon the engine could be seen. Now to clean the spillage from around it, and its frame. Once this was done, it was time for the bar trick! Put the one-inch diameter, five-foot-long steel bar over the top of the tailpiece extension of the engine, then drive the bottom end of the bar through the spillage and under the frame. The bar was now like a stir stick that was put over one side of a doughnut and under the other side. Then Sparky and I stood on the bar with our backs pressing the roof and pushed like hell with our legs.

If enough spillage had been removed, the frame would lift a foot or so out of the remaining spillage. It did! We were on our way. The same "bait and pry" trick loosened the front end of the engine. The loosened engine was then pried, inches at a time, almost to the coal face. It could not go right to the coal face, because a place had to be prepared for it. Fred now started to shovel duff from the coal face and throw it where the engine used to be. The three of us were getting pretty tired by now, but there was a lot of work to be done yet.

Now we had to dig a "bed" in the pavement next to the coal face. All the coal had to be removed from the pavement until we reached solid stone. If the engine was set up on coal, the pounding pan line would crumble the coal under the engine, the timber would loosen, and the engine would slide downhill and quit. Better to deal with the devil than management if that happened. Fred, Sparky and I took turns digging.

Its bed prepared, the engine was now pried the rest of the way to the face and into the bed. Fred held a shovel under the sharp corners of the frame so it would not dig into the pavement, and I pried with the bar. The engine moved only inches at a time. Finally, we "put it to bed." Now we bulled the drive pan in place and hooked the engine piston to it. Then, with no pans yet on top of the engine, Fred started timbering the face side. Three timber—two straight up from the face side corners of the frame to the roof. Then the face side "sprag"—a timber angled against the frame at about forty-five degrees to keep the engine from sliding downhill.

Now, a "saddle roller" was put on top of the engine, and the pan that was to go over the engine was set on this roller. This avoided friction between the pan and the engine. Sparky and I shifted three more pans, the last of which joined Number Two pan line, while Fred timbered the gob side of the engine.

Once finished, Fred put the engine on short stroke, hooked the two-inch air hose to it, and crawled to the air valve to gently start the pan line. The timbered engine had to hold about five thousand pounds of pans from slipping downhill. He let it run for a minute. It went: "PIToo, PIToo, PIToo...," and the empty pans clunked as they reached the limit of the down stroke, and were jerked quickly upwards again. If the timbering were not solid to the roof, the pans would pull the engine downhill and it would quit. However, the engine didn't move, which was always the case when Fred timbered it. Time to go home. Thank gawd! We were very tired, and the wind had the eyes burning out of our heads.

# 4

# The Gob

AFTER A FEW MONTHS, pan shifting developed
into a regular routine for me, but not really a welcome
routine. I was six foot two inches tall, and things were
good if there were four feet of height on the gob side of
the pans, which was where I was supposed to be for the
first lift on the pan. Really no problem if the pan could
come straight sideways to the face—Fred and I would
simply jerk it out from the face side. Once out from the
gob, I could step on the other side, and we were ready
to heave. If, however, the pan had to go up or down,
which was mostly the case, one of us had to be on each
side of the thing, which meant that I had to get on the
gob side, no matter how cramped the space there.

About this time, I was beginning to contemplate
my future. Sure as hell, I did not want to be a pan
shifter much longer. I had to start making plans for an
easier job. I was young and in good shape, but this was
damn hard work!—and for sure, I was not pleased
with the prospects of doing it for more than a year or
so. Fact was, however, that is all I knew how to do—
common, simple labour. I decided to improve my skills
by going to night school. Electrician seemed like a nice
job, so I signed up for night classes for mine electrician. It was interesting, and I enjoyed it. I wasn't a

mole, and I didn't feel like working like one. Perhaps some day I would be able to stand up and work like a man doing electrical work.

In the meantime, I often looked at the gob workers. They could stand at least partially straight, and work in the gob. I wondered if that would be an easier job. I would soon get a chance to find out.

We knew all of the gob workers on Number One pan line—six of them—two to each of the fifty-foot gob sections: Albert and Louie; Dan and Bobby; Frank and "?" It was Frank and "?" because Frank had lost his steady buddy, and had a new one about every day. Frank had been looking for a steady buddy for quite a while. We knew this, because the pan engine was in Frank's section, and we spent most of the shift at the engine, so we talked to Frank a lot.

Frank was a beautiful person—older, Polish descent, polite and sociable. Everyone liked Frank, and respected him. One day Frank suggested that I come to be his buddy in the gob. On first thought, I dismissed the idea; but it never left me. Before the shift was over, I had second thoughts. The gob side of the pans was not getting any roomier, and the drive pan and the engine were not getting any lighter. In the face of this, Frank would be a nice person to work with, and his section was the best on the wall.

When we got to the engine that day, we decided to shift the drive pan before lunch. After brute bulling the drive pan in place, we sat down to eat. As usual, we saw Frank, and he brought the subject up again. If Frank really wanted me, he couldn't have asked at a better time. Still sweating from shifting the drive pan, I said: "Okay, Frank, if they say I can go, I will." I was sure management would not let me go from the pan shifting crew, because it was hard to get steady pan shifters in 18 West. I was wrong. Frank asked, and management agreed. A day or so later, I got the news. I had a new job: working in the gob.

WHEN I TOLD SOMEONE I was a pan shifter, I felt a little more pride than when I told them I was working "in the gob." However, a gob worker was more important than a pan shifter. If the pan shifters screwed up, the wall would be tied up for a while, but it would get right back into routine production again. Not so with the gob, because as the gob sections went, so went the conditions of the wall. If the gob workers did not do it right, the roof conditions of the wall would deteriorate and become more dangerous. If the roof came in, or was threatening to do so, the wall would go slow for days, or production could stop altogether.

Simply put, the gob was the place in a coal mine where the coal used to be. After the coal was taken, the roof over all that area was *supposed* to cave in—a controlled fall. If it did not cave in, conditions on the face began to worsen. The gob worker was supposed to support the roof over the working area close to the wall face, and also allow the roof to cave in beginning about twenty feet back from the coal face. This cave-in part was my introduction to the real danger in coal mining, but I could not have had a better person to train me in gob work. Frank knew the gob well, and did his job right. It showed. The wall was nowhere in better shape than at Frank's section.

IT WAS ABOUT THIS TIME that another interest came into my life—a neat little young woman who lived just about a mile up the road from me. She was pretty, with curves in all the right places. I had met her when I worked at Eaton's. She was still working there. One day I decided I would give her a twirl. I went back to Eaton's and met her—by accident, of course. She was still unattached, so I talked to her for as long as I could get away with. Before I left, I asked: "What's your phone number?" The little smart ass answered: "Cucumber." I went back again the next day to buy "something," and asked for her number again. She must have decided that I was not all that bad, so she gave me her phone number. That was the start of something that was to change both our lives. Her name was Norma.

MY FIRST SHIFT IN THE GOB was one where we had to draw five gob-side chucks and build them again, along with two more, between the pan line and the coal face. A chuck was a two-and-a-half-foot square pillar from the pavement (floor) to the roof, built with hardwood blocks. "Drawing" a chuck meant taking it down. As it was now at the start of the shift, there were two rows of chucks on the gob side of the pans, for the full fifty feet of gob section. It was like two rows on a checkerboard—the five back-line chucks were in between, and behind, the front-line ones.

The work was still brutal—interesting because it was different from pan shifting, but still brutal. There was never enough room to stand up and work like a man. However, the relationship with pretty little Norma was blossoming, so I worked my proverbial ass off. It was no longer just me and the coal mine—no longer just a job! It was a means to provide for a possible home life with a lovely little woman. That possibility gave me strength that I never thought I had. Norma could never know the work I was doing, but now I was doing it for her! The blocks used to build the chucks were six inches square and two and a half feet long. They weighed about forty pounds each. I threw them around now like a macho maniac, fantasizing that Norma was watching. As far as brain work went, however, it was not that impressive. It was only brawn.

Building a chuck was exactly the same idea as building a small square tower with popsicle sticks. Put two sticks down in a right-left direction, parallel, and the length of the sticks away from each other. Then two more crosswise on top of these at each end, and so on up. There was one major, but simple, difference. When it came to the third set of blocks, laid the same direction as the first set, the gob side, or furthest-away block, had to be moved six inches in from the ends of the blocks under it. This was the "trip" block. This meant that the ends of the next two blocks on top of the trip block extended over the trip block by six inches, the same as the two blocks under the trip block. Then it was straight popsicle-stick tower building up to the roof.

My mind was preoccupied with my girl friend, and pleasantly so. I could think of nothing else. This weekend, we were going to pick blueberries—alone. Geez! That had possibilities. My mind went into each possibility with pleasure but, simple as it was, I had to keep some of my mind for the work in front of me.

Should I forget to put this one, lonely, very important trip block six inches in from all the rest, I was doomed to the coal miner's hall of infamy, because I would have built a "square" chuck. This was not a compliment. There would be no way to relieve the tremendous pressure squeezing this square chuck be-

tween the roof and the pavement. It would be like trying to get a jack out from under a loaded dump truck
without first letting the truck down on its wheels.
Whoever had to draw a square chuck was in for a very
bad day. With every swing of the maul, the guy would
be saying: "What *#@!&% stupid bastard built this?!"

Frank made sure I knew about the trip block,
then set me to building chucks. Since the last coal
shift, there was now a four-and-a-half-foot space between the pans and the whole length of the coal face.
Each gob team had to support their own fifty feet of
this space. It was done by building seven chucks along
the coal face, each one about five feet from the other.

The first two chucks were built with loose blocks
that were saved for that purpose from the last shift—
about forty-five or fifty blocks. I took the blocks from
where Frank had them stacked, and put them on the
pan line, intending to simply step over the pan line
and begin building my chuck, taking blocks from the
pan line as needed. Not a good idea! Blocks were too
precious. Frank pointed out to me that somebody
might be sending some machinery or some material
down the wall, and using the pan line to do it. If my
blocks were piled on the pan line when it started,
away went the blocks!

The last thing any gob worker wanted was to
carry blocks. Even to replace one block was a lot of
work. I would have to crawl down the wall about 150
feet, then a bent-over walk out the level even farther,
find a block, carry it back to the bottom of the wall,
then toss it ahead of me a few feet at a time until I
reached my section. If the pan line started with blocks
on it, it was panic time getting them off before they
disappeared down the wall. To replace enough blocks

to build two chucks would take most of the shift. I took the blocks off the pan line.

More than once, a fight would break out over blocks. Sometimes, when a gob worker needed just one or two blocks to finish the shift, the temptation was to steal them from another section, especially if the team in that section had finished and gone home. They had better not steal any from Frank's section. Frank marked all his blocks by clipping off their eight corners. A bit of work for about 200 blocks, but it was just one swing of the axe for each corner. No one wanted to be caught with Frank's blocks, not because Frank would get physical, but because everyone respected Frank so much. Then again, once I got to know Frank, I would not be surprised to see Frank tearing down someone else's chuck if he saw one of his own blocks there. Frank was no pussycat. No one was going to walk over him.

AGAIN I WISHED Norma could see me now, and the work I was doing. It was simple labour, but the conditions under which it was done made it something to be proud of. This place was more than two miles underground—dark, dusty, dangerous, and extremely cramped—a human being should not really be here, but her boy friend was, throwing hardwood blocks around in an attempt to make a good life for both of them. If she could see me now she would think of me as a brave hero. Fantasizing her watching me made the work much easier. When I thought of her, the blocks became lighter and easier to lift.

I CLEARED AWAY THE DUFF, and built two chucks beside the coal face with the loose blocks saved for that purpose. Now, five more chucks had to be built above these, and in line with them at five-foot intervals. This gob work was every bit as hard as shifting pans. Building a chuck took a lot of lifting and carrying the blocks. Dear gawd—what a beautiful bum on Norma!

Once close to the roof, the thing had to be wedged solid. Finding wedges was no party, because they were supposed to be small and made of hardwood. Yah, sure! Forget the hardwood part. If management wanted hardwood wedges, they could friggin' well supply them. The only hardwood around here were these blocks, and for damn sure, no one was going to start hand sawing them into small enough pieces to make wedges. Management knew that, but it was another "blind eye" thing. However, if the underground manager saw a large piece of softwood timber being used for a wedge, he would make me take it out, and pick at the roof coal until I had room for a full-sized hardwood block as tight as I could get it against the roof.

Management was strict on the wedging of the chucks—they had to be tight to the roof. The mine manager himself came down the pan line one day, checking all the tops of the chucks for proper and solid wedging, actually pulling at some of the freshly-set wedges. Not all were to his liking. Not thinking of what he was saying, he said right out loud: "These chucks should be built from the roof down so the blocks can be tight to the roof!" only to say a few seconds later: "Oh geez, what am I saying?" The point was made, however: he wanted these chucks wedged solid!

Now things began to get serious. In order to get blocks to build five more chucks, they had to draw the five back-line chucks—those farthest in the gob. This is where it got a bit dangerous. These chucks were holding up the roof, and they had to come out! The roof behind them, in the gob, had no support. It often happened that when a chuck was being drawn, the roof behind it was just waiting to fall, and when it did, took the roof over the freshly-drawn chuck with it, burying those blocks. Then, with one eye on the roof, Frank and I had to work like hell to shovel those blocks out from under the fall.

Frank would not let me take the whole chuck out on my first shift in the gob. He let me do only the first part. The first part in drawing a chuck was that the face-side, bottom block had to be laboriously dug under with a pick, so it could drop a bit—two inches at the most—definitely not enough to loosen the whole chuck, but enough to loosen it a bit, so the blocks could be pounded out. Once this bottom block was dropped a bit, the pounding started in earnest with an eight-pound maul. There was tremendous pressure on these blocks, and none of them came out without severe, laborious pounding. This first bottom block was no exception.

Once the bottom block was out, *really* start pounding! The face-side ends of the two blocks on top of the bottom one had to be pounded in toward each other. Then the two "wing" blocks above these had to be pounded out, away from each other. Then the back of the chuck, hopefully, collapsed into the empty six-inch space behind the trip block. Sometimes the blocks would fly out suddenly, like a wet orange seed that was pressed between thumb and finger. The gob worker had to be ready to move quickly to avoid a pussful of flying blocks.

Hard as it was, the pounding was not the toughest problem—the problem was, there was never enough room to get a good swing with the maul. The chuck would have yielded quickly to our efforts had we been able to stand up, take the maul by the end of the handle, and then bring it down from behind the shoulder and onto the block. Forget that dream. Half a swing was the rule, and that while on our knees. A lot of the time, it was more of a long push with the maul instead of a hearty swing.

Frank let me dig under the bottom block, then pound it and the other blocks until the chuck was about to loosen. Then he took over. When the blocks began to loosen, Frank got cautious. No longer would he stand close to the chuck and swing away at it. When it looked like the chuck was ready to collapse, he would hold on to one of the solid chucks on the front line with one hand, and jab at the loose blocks with the end of the maul handle from a safe distance. This chuck was under roof pressure, and now was about to come down. Maybe a lot of roof would come down with it. If that were the case, Frank was not going to be under it—nor was I.

Not bad this time. The chuck collapsed, but the roof stayed. Still, Frank would not venture into the gob to retrieve the loose blocks. Instead, he took the miner's pick, and from relative safety in between two front-line chucks, he reached in and swung the pick, sticking it into the side of a block, close to its end. Then he simply pulled the block out of the gob with the pick. I took each block out of the way, as Frank pulled block after block out of the gob. Once we got all the blocks out, Frank showed me where to set them up again on the face side of the pans. While I was building a new chuck on the face, Frank was drawing another one in the gob. Finally, all five back-line chucks were drawn, and all seven face-side chucks were built. Now there were fourteen chucks in all: seven on each side of the pan line. It was now time for the most awesome and fearful event of the entire coal mining industry—the cutting of the gob.

EVEN THE MOST SEASONED COAL MINERS profoundly respected a gob "coming in." For the ones who had built the roof-supporting chucks, there was always an instant of doubt when the roof let go. "Did we do everything right?" If the chucks they built rolled out, it was game over! This time, however, I didn't know enough to be worried. When shifting pans, I had never been right beside a gob section when the gob was cut. Frank put me on the pan line and told me to stay there.

There were five or six timber still standing in the gob. These had to be chopped until they cracked and bent in the middle, so they were no longer holding up any roof. Frank shone his light on the timber farthest in the gob. It had to be cut. He listened and looked carefully for any sign of "spitting"—small amounts of stone that fell as warning that the roof was "working"—getting ready to cave in. No spitting, so Frank stepped into the unsupported gob as far as he dare go, then leaned toward the timber and swung the axe with one extended arm, drawing back immediately and listening again. His decision was that it was safe enough for another swing—and another. After three or four good chops to the side of the timber, it cracked. Frank was out of the gob instantly, and kneeling on the pan line with me.

No one had to listen and watch for spitting now—

it was obvious: this gob was going to "come in." The whole section was restless and working. Frank knew that the rest of the timber did not have to be cut. They would soon snap like toothpicks. He was right. In just a few seconds, it was like the roof of the whole fifty-foot section was a full and frozen giant ice cube tray that someone had tipped upside down and twisted. There was a violent, vicious cracking and snapping of the remaining timber, then a thunderous, vibrating, crashing roar.

The roof fell like the proverbial ton of bricks—tons and tons and tons of bricks. Cold stonedust whooshed and charged from the gob like from a bomb blast, totally blinding us. I was terrified. I wanted to run—but where? It seemed like the whole world was falling. Thankfully, it was over in a few seconds. When the dust cleared, I shone my light between the gob side chucks. It was no longer a large, empty, dark room. There *was* no room. Now there was a wall of grey stone right to the back of the gob-side chucks. I wondered if they always held. If they didn't, would Norma be sad for me?

EVERY SO OFTEN, my hearing would go dim. What's wrong!? Not to worry, I was told, it is just coal dust. Go to the doctor and get your ears syringed out. No problem. But it was not the breeze it was made out to be. The medical staff was not gentle. For a procedure like this, it was just a cut above a veterinarian's office. They didn't even bother to heat the water. Just filled a stainless-steel syringe with cold water, shoved it in the ear canal, and drove the water in. It sounded ten times louder than Niagara Falls, and felt like it. Gawd help the poor guy whose ears were really plugged.

## The Gob

Big, tough coal miners didn't whine or lament—
they just took it. If their buddies found out they even
winced, there would be no living it down. You'd be
called a baby and a wimp, and a whole lot worse.

The first time I had this done, I was amazed at
the amount of black lumps that came out of my ear. In
any event, three blasts in each ear usually did the
trick—hearing restored.

NORMA AND I went picking blueberries that weekend. It was a beautiful day, and there was a brisk
breeze, which made it even more beautiful, because
Norma was wearing a long, thin cotton dress. When
she stood up straight, the wind blew it around and between her legs—nice! I wished she would turn around
and let the wind blow on her back, but she knelt down
and kept facing the blueberries. When we came back
to her house we made blueberry pie, and had a lovely
evening. When we kissed good night, however, I ca-
ressed that part of her that she would not let the wind
blow on. Wow!

ALTHOUGH IT SOUNDED AND FELT like the gob
came in for the whole length of the wall, it didn't—nor
could it be allowed to, because each gob worker had to
be in control of his own fifty-foot section. It was a very
impressive cave-in, but it was only Frank's fifty feet of
gob that caved in, because there were "dummy" walls
every fifty feet, and at right angles to the coal face.
These were miner-made walls that reached back as
far as the gob went—back to where the wall face first
started to be mined at the main deep.

Every second day, each dummy wall had to be extended toward the coal face. They were twelve feet

wide, and had to be extended nine feet—the width of the coal that was missing—the coal that was taken out during two production, or "coal," shifts. My second shift in the gob, therefore, was a dummy-wall day. The shifts alternated between a chuck-drawing day and a dummy-wall day. The dummy-wall day was definitely not as dramatic as a chuck-drawing day. It was just as laborious, but not as dramatic, since the gob was not cut and the roof did not fall.

On a dummy-wall day, Frank and I drew only two chucks—the two that we left standing in front of the dummy wall. The dummy wall was going to be built where these two chucks were. We did not rebuild these two chucks, but stored the blocks between the remaining five chucks on the gob side of the pans. These blocks would be used again tomorrow. Today was "dummy day." It was going to be a good dummy day, because there was lots of stone—the gob came in as it should. Still, however, we had to shovel enough stone to fill a twelve-by-nine-by-five-foot area, if that can be called a "good" day.

A "bad" dummy-wall day was one after the gob had not come in—the roof had not fallen, and there was no stone to build the dummy wall extension. Sometimes the gob did not come in for two or three shifts. In that case, we would have to venture back into the unsupported gob to the last place where it did come in—perhaps twenty feet or more under unsupported roof—dangerous territory.

Usually Frank accepted the dangerous part, going into the gob to the stone. He'd shovel the stone to me, and then I would shovel it into the dummy wall. A long, hard shift when that happened. There were instances where the gob did not come in for four or five gob-cutting shifts, which meant that anyone building a dummy wall in that section, and wanting stone for it, would have to go under unsupported roof for fifty feet or more. No one in their right mind would take that chance. Consequently, any coal, or anything else that they could find to throw into the dummy wall, went in, and to hell with the stone, even though the dummy wall was supposed to be filled with stone only! This is what management wanted, but that is not always what they got! When there was no stone, anything that could be found went into the dummy wall.

A story has it that one gob team somehow got hold of an empty 45-gallon oil drum. In it went, and it was covered with duff as quickly as possible. Unfortunately for them, the underground manager was just coming down the pan line checking the dummy walls. He had a wooden cane for that purpose. He would push the cane in between the lumps of stone that made up the outside wall of the dummy to check if the twelve-by-nine-by-five-foot space inside the wall was indeed full to the roof. The end of a wooden cane hitting stone has its own sound. An empty oil drum also has its own sound. The guys had to tear down their dummy wall, remove the drum, and do it right.

WHEN FRANK AND I STARTED a dummy wall, Frank would shovel a trench in the duff where the new dummy wall was to be built. The trench started at the low side corner of the existing dummy wall, and went nine feet to the pans, then twelve feet up along the gob side of the pans, then nine feet over again to the high side corner of the existing dummy wall. While Frank was shoveling, I was getting the biggest pieces of stone I could lift, laying them along Frank's trench. Then it was just like laying bricks, only using large, jagged pieces of stone. We would build the wall up a foot or so, then shovel stone inside the wall. When the shoveled stone reached the top of the stacked stone, we would build up more wall, and so on until the stacked stone reached the roof, and we could not shovel in any more stone.

A few more stacked stone to cover the last opening through which we shoveled, and we were finished. The underground manager could shove his cane through the holes in this wall, and he would hit only stone. This was Frank's section—and it was done right.

Home time, and I looked forward to spending more time with Norma. We were getting thicker. It really looked like we would be an item. For me, everything was more beautiful and more meaningful. I was sure that Norma, working at Eaton's, felt the same about me. Nice!

# 5

# Extra Shift

THE WORK WAS HARD, and the pay was small. I was making about twelve dollars a day. In those days, the office would deduct income tax and the like from a miner's pay, and also any payments requested by the miner—even church donations. I had them take off every payment I was supposed to make. After deductions, I would take home about thirty-five dollars a week—just on the low side of enough, especially now that Norma and I were thinking of getting married.

Even one missed shift was quite a financial strain. There was no work for me each Monday when the production shift was night shift, which was every second week. The pit did not produce coal on Saturday or Sunday. Consequently, when Frank and I maintained our gob section on Friday night shift, it stayed that way until Monday night shift when the loaders came down. After the loaders had the wall cleaned off on night shift, it had to be undermined again with the Samson cutting machine on back shift. This machine pulled itself down the wall while cutting a four-and-a-half-foot-long cut under the coal face with a giant chain saw, or jib, that protruded at right angles from the machine.

The Samson was the machine that made all the

duff along the face. There would be no chucks built close to the face until this machine did its work. That meant Monday was a down day as far as gob work was concerned. I could have taken the day off, but that was no way to build an economic base for my love life. On these Mondays, I was determined to find a shift somewhere else.

On my first try, I really lucked out. I got a shift on my own wall—18 West—and in Frank's gob section! The air valve for Number One pan engine—the engine I used to help move—was in Frank's gob section, and I was to be valve tender for that shift.

This was the easiest shift I had so far. All I had to do was open and close the valve to start and stop the engine. This was the same valve that had accidentally opened on Sput the day he was over-anxious to test the stability of the engine we had just shifted. No such disastrous consequence today. I had a two-foot length of pipe that I slipped over the short valve handle. This gave me good control when opening the valve. All I had to do now was stay alert enough to see a light waving when the Sydney Mines Loader stopped, so I would stop the pan line, then catch the same signal again when the Sydney Mines Loader started, so I could start the pan line. It was a piece of cake. This was my first time on the "coal" shift, and a good shift it was. I was sorry when it was over.

Usually, I was quite tired and ready for home after a shift in the gob. Today, however, the valve-tending cakewalk left me not in the least tired. This surplus energy would soon be put to good use. Word came down that the 17 West overman was looking for a timber carrier. I thought an extra shift would be nice, so I volunteered. Had I known, I would have saved some lunch for this next shift, but I thought: "Just a few hours to get the timber down the wall, then go flake out somewhere until home time." Wrong! No damn wonder the 17 West overman was looking for a timber carrier! No one was stupid enough to take the job. He was *always* looking for a timber carrier.

The coal came out the bottom of 17 West on the "slant" level—17 West "main" level went to the top of 17 West wall and was used only for timber, other materials, and ventilation. Like a sheep to the slaughter, I went in 17 West main level at the top of the wall to start carrying timber.

Dear gawd! What a mess! This level was a new word for "clutter." It was wide enough for boxes (coal cars) only, and the roof was only about a foot above the boxes. This small space made it difficult even to get the timber out of the boxes. Worse: on both sides of the road were huge, ugly timber—ones that timber carriers gave up on without even trying. They just rolled them out of the boxes, left them there, and reached for smaller ones. There was no hope of walking over these discarded timber alongside the boxes. They were stacked too high.

Worse—infinitely worse!—was something I should have known, but never thought about: 17 West had a gundy hole, and the ventilating air in 17 West was worse than anywhere else in the pit. In that gundy hole, the wind was vicious. If you threw a shovel in there, it would blow back. The stage was set for one helluva hard shift. The valve tending was easy, but this would more than make up for it. No decent, self-respecting miner would offer himself for a shift here unless he was desperate.

Consequently, Sawdust was to be my partner.

This guy was a character. I did not know why they called him Sawdust. I thought maybe it was because he slept and snored when he should have been working. I was to find out later that Sawdust was suspected of stealing food from other guys' lunch cans when they weren't looking. If he tried to rob my can tonight, he was out of luck, because it was long since empty. Whatever, Sawdust was definitely no ball of fire. He didn't talk much—just grinned. As long as he could carry timber, I really didn't give a damn. About 200 six-foot timber had to get down the wall, a lot of them twice as heavy as usual, and slippery because of the snow and ice frozen to them. I sure wanted Sawdust to carry his share.

The shift started badly—we had to wait for timber. It must have been close to two hours before the boxes arrived. The loaders were already pissed off. Each loader was supposed to get eight timber, and it was well past time for their first two timber. However, the boxes were here now and it was timber-carrying time. With the limited space above the boxes, it was tough enough just to get the timber out of the first box and on its way to the gundy hole. But there were four boxes, one behind the other, each with timber in them. You couldn't just take timber from the second box and walk alongside the boxes to the front of the trip. There was no room to walk next to the boxes. The timber carrier had to get *in* the box and wrestle each timber from the second box into the first one, and then out the front. Then from the third box, into the second box, into the first box, and out in front. Same for the fourth box. Geez! That was a shift in itself!

Then, the gundy hole! Sawdust and I struggled to pile about fifty timber at the top side of the gundy—

two timber for each of the loaders. Then the timber had to go through that friggin' hole. This was the absolute worst part of the shift. I tossed two timber into the hole, then it was a hands-and-knees crawl through the roughly twenty feet of gundy hole, pushing the timber ahead. From this cramped hands-and-knees position, there was no way I could put my left hand under the middle of the timber, lift, then heave with my right hand. The timber could not be lifted at all—it had to be pushed from the top end. If it caught in the pavement, which it often did, it had to be turned and pushed at the same time so it would roll over whatever it was caught on. The particles dug up by the front end of the timber were drilled by the wind like stone hailstones into my pit helmet. I didn't dare lift my face into that vicious wind. Sawdust did the same. It took a long time to get those fifty timber through the gundy hole two at a time. I thought, no human being should ever have to do this for a living, but there was no backing out now.

Once through the gundy, we had to carry the timber another hundred feet or so to the top of the wall, and put them on the pan line. The loaders took them off. Sometimes we tried backing into the gundy and pulling the timber in after us, but this was slower, since one timber was all we could manage at a time. It was impossible to pull a timber to your kneecaps, then reach over it to grab the end of another timber above it. You would have to lie on top of the timber you had just pulled into the hole. Very uncomfortable! That damn gundy hole was just too small.

All this was plenty bad enough—but Sawdust made it even worse! I still wonder about that guy. On one trip back up through the gundy for more timber,

Sawdust went ahead of me. We were crawling in the same direction as the wind now. Both of us were in the gundy, and I was crawling like hell to get out of it, but I caught up to Sawdust. For some reason, Sawdust stopped in front of me. I thought: "Why in hell would anyone stop in a place like this?" I looked at the soles of Sawdust's pit boots, then looked up a bit.

There, looking back at me eye to eye was Sawdust's dirty, ugly, very bare, coal-dust-ringed arsehole. The seam of his pants was torn from belt to balls, and he had no shorts on! I roared several very uncomplimentary expletives at Sawdust, punched him on the right side of his arse, and roared at him again to move! He did.

Once out of the gundy, I asked Sawdust why he had stopped. He didn't answer—just smiled a sly smile. Damn wierdo! After this, I was sure to be the first one in the gundy hole. When that shift was over, I never wanted to see Sawdust or another timber again.

ONE THING I MISSED DEARLY: when I went out with Norma, I could not talk to her about these things. There was simply no way she could understand, because she never saw these conditions, nor would she ever see them. The only person I could tell these stories to was another coal miner, and I sure as hell did not want another coal miner on my date with my girl friend. So we talked about Eaton's. Then again, for a lot of the evening, we did not have to talk at all. We could communicate our feelings quite nicely without words. Beautiful!

# 6

# Loading Coal

AFTER THAT EXTRA SHIFT I stayed away from carrying timber. It was the least-paid job in the pit, and definitely not the least work. The problem was, day shift Monday every second week, there was no work for Frank and me in the gob. And there were not that many other shifts to be had except for carrying timber or loading coal.

I had never asked for a section of coal before, because I was afraid to ask—afraid I would get what I asked for. Aside from brushing—which was loading stone—loading coal was the hardest work in the pit. I had done it one time, but only for about fifteen or twenty minutes when I gave a loader a "run"—that is, loaded coal for him to give him a rest and a chance to eat. When the run was over, I was spent. I was glad I did not have to do that for the whole shift, and I often wondered if I could.

A section of coal was eighteen and a half feet long and as many tons—one ton a foot. Loading it was not all that had to be done. The section had to be "duffed," meaning that the loose coal had to be cleaned out of the four-inch by four-and-a-half-foot mining slot that was cut under the whole length of the section—the whole length of the wall, in fact. If this slot was packed with loose duff, the coal could not be shot down properly. It would mean too much work with the pick.

Like everything else in the pit, duffing was not the problem—getting the duffing shovel under the coal face *was* a problem. The pans were tight to the face, and there were chucks against the other side of the pans. There never was enough room to make the work just natural work! Even getting to the work was work. Besides duffing the section, the loader also had to put up four timbered straps as supports once the supporting coal was loaded away.

I considered all this with a mixture of fear and adventure. This particular Monday morning, adventure took over. I had been in the pit for about a year now, was in good shape, and knew what it was like to work hard. I decided to take the plunge. I nervously approached the 19 West production overman and asked for a section of coal. The overman didn't make matters any easier, because he asked: "Are you sure you can do it?" I almost backed out, but nodded: "Yes." I lied, because I was not sure. The overman wasn't sure either. But on Monday mornings there were usually some loaders who didn't report for work because of a hangover. The overman was desperate.

My stomach shot about a gallon of adrenaline when he said: "Okay—take the third section from the bottom. The gear is buried along the high side of the dummy wall." The gear was a pan shovel, pick, duffing shovel, axe, and handsaw. I gave the overman my check number, went to the pick house for a can of powder, and headed for an early rake. No turning back now! I was excited, nervous and scared all at the same time. Whatever this shift would be like, it would not be boring. This was big-league stuff.

## Loading Coal

NOT ALL HUNG-OVER LOADERS stayed home. These guys were tough—they literally worked off their hangovers. Sometimes they also shared their hangover with a rake full of men. After consuming beer, salami, pepperoni, kolbassa, and heaven knows what other spicy foods, they came to work. One such guy sat at the very bottom section of the rake, waiting for it to start down. He then blew a murderous, billowing, black "whodunnit" fart. Then he sat there with a grin, knowing full well what would happen in the next few seconds. Thanks to the ventilating air, his predictions came true with a "gawd DAMN!" Then: "BASTARD!" And frequent use of the usual four-letter word. From the waist up, each miner in the rake above the silent offender tipped outward like toppling dominoes, trying to get his nose out of the airstream. Thankfully, the ventilating air made short work of his hangover contribution. He was smiling now, but wait until the poor bugger started loading coal!

I GOT DOWN TO THE ASSIGNED SECTION—third from the bottom. This was really the third worst section on the wall. There would be at least seventeen loaders above me, which meant there would be precious little room for me to shovel coal onto the pan line. With seventeen seasoned loaders above me, all heaving coal onto it, the pan line would be very full at the bottom end. However, this did not really matter to me, because I knew I would be slow anyway. As a matter of fact, a forced slow pace would be in my favour. The way it worked was that when the pan line started, the loaders loaded like hell until the trip of coal cars under the chute was loaded, and the pan line stopped. Then everyone waited until another empty trip was brought in. Each loader heaved what coal he could onto the pan line while he had the chance. I was sure I could not keep up a pace like that. If I had to wait a bit to get my coal on—fine!

I found the gear right where the overman said it would be. As simple as it was, a miner had to be careful when digging for his gear. I'd heard this story: At home time this day, one miner was burying his gear while another turned out his light and secretly watched. His gear safely buried, that miner went home, but the miner who was secretly watching took a crap right on top of where the gear was buried. Then he covered his deposit with more duff. When the miner who owned the gear came to start his next shift, he dug with his bare hands for the gear. Obviously, he came to the deposit before he came to his gear. Once he stirred it up and realized from the scent what was on his fingers, he held out both his hands and whined: "Cut them off—cut them off!"

I used a broken wooden wedge to dig for the gear.

The duffing shovel was to be my first tool. It was a flat piece of steel about a foot square, with a long handle. It was not dished like an ordinary shovel because it had to be pushed under the coal face into the narrow space cut out by the Samson machine. This was the part I worried about. This was the first cut. On the second cut there was four and a half feet between the pan line and the coal face. There was room to work the duffing shovel. But on this first cut, the pans were tight against the face. I had to work from under the pans! I had to lie on my belly on the gob side of the pans, and push the duffing shovel into the mining from there. Not really a problem if there did not happen to be a chuck against the pans every five feet. But there was! So if there were no pan wheels and cradle in the way, there was a two-and-a-half-foot-square chuck in the way.

Geez! To get the duff out from under the whole section was going to take too much time, and in a few minutes those pans were going to be moving. I started to panic and sweat. I was too excited. If I didn't get control of myself, I would never make it. I started to reason: "Hey, just duff under the first hole, shoot it down, load the coal, and then duff the next hole from where that coal used to be." That's what I would do! There were eight holes—four bottom and four top. So for now, I just duffed the one low-side bottom hole. I knew I was working too hard, and sweating too much. I was too excited to settle down. By the time I got this first hole duffed, the rest of the loaders were down and the wall was ready to start.

As I had heard loaders do before, I roared: "Shot-fire!" I had heard no one shout this ahead of me, so this put me first in line for the shotfirer to come to my section and fire the first bottom hole. I gave the shotfirer a plug of blasting powder, into which he shoved a quarter-inch round spike-shaped brass rod. He then put a blasting cap into the hole it made, and wrapped the cap wire around the plug of powder. Then, after cleaning out the hole in the face, he rammed the powder into the hole with a "stemmer"—a long piece of wood like a broom handle. Two cap wires trailed this plug of powder into the back end of the hole, and were long enough to protrude from the front, coal face end, of the hole. The shotfirer's cable was connected to these cap wires. Then another plug and a half of powder. The hole was then filled with clay, and coal "helpers." The entire length of the hole was supposed to be filled with clay only, but who in hell is going to carry down that much clay, or spend that much time plugging the entire hole with clay? So, shove some coal in there to "help."

Once the hole was ready to be "shot," the shotfirer went up the wall twenty feet or so, and I went down the wall the same distance. Then we both shouted "fire!" as loud as we could, and the shotfirer twisted the handle on his small dynamo, sending an electric current into the blasting cap. "Whump!" The powder went. The first, and worst, hole was fired.

The shotfirer yanked his cable out of the shot-down coal and went to the next section. I went to view the results. Some of the coal was blasted onto the pan line—good!—but now to load the rest.

This first heap of coal was a hard one, because it was loose coal in the middle of a solid wall of coal. I had to get through the loosened coal to the pavement. This was the smooth bottom where the pan shovel would slide easily into the pile of coal, and the coal would almost fall onto the shovel. However, until I got to the pavement, I had to drive the pan shovel into the side of the pile and scoop what I could onto the pan line. This was hard, gut-wrenching work—bad enough for a seasoned loader, but this was my first section of coal, and I was uptight and tense. I was pushing myself too hard. The tension was making me sweat more than the coal. I made it to the pavement, but I had used up too much energy, and now, the loading started in earnest. It was me and the pan shovel now!

The pan shovel was also known as the "banjo." A lot of guys called it the "back breaker," because of its size. An ordinary garden shovel is about nine inches wide and twelve inches from the shoulder to the point. A pan shovel is sixteen and a half inches wide by eighteen inches, with no shoulder. It is almost round with a three-foot handle. That's why the name "banjo."

After I got almost all the loose coal onto the pan line, I roared again: "Shotfire!" By the time I had loaded all the coal from the first hole, the shotfirer appeared again to shoot the hole above the first one. This hole was different. There was about three feet of empty space below it now. Just one plug of powder— even half a plug—was all that was needed. The loader made this decision. Too much powder, and I had to work harder to shovel smaller coal. Not enough and I would have to "work my arse off" with the pick to get the coal down. Then I would probably leave an "overhang"—coal still stuck to the face—for which I would get hell. Just the right amount, however, and I had all the coal down in nice-sized lumps. Much easier. I put one full plug in this hole—too much.

Once again the shotfirer went up the wall, and I went down to warn of the shot to be fired. We both hollered "fire," then "WHACK" went this hole, and the sound of coal falling. There wasn't enough coal to muffle this shot. This meant the coal would be small. Okay, so be it—chalk it up to the greenhorn. I went at it and soon had it all on the pan line—but I was getting tired.

Previous to this, I had taken timber off the pan line and thrown them in the gob. Now was the time to use them. I had loaded about one-third of my section, now the roof had to be supported with a timber and a strap where that coal once was. I had put up timber before, but never a "strap." A strap was simply another timber, only laid across the roof, with a timber under the end where the coal used to be, and the other end into a "stayhole" dug into the coal face. This "stayhole" was only about four inches in diameter and three inches into the coal face, but it was no small matter for me.

I had watched miners dig them before, and it looked easy, but looks were deceiving. The hole had to be dug into the very solid coal just where the roof and the coal face met. I drove the pick into the coal where I wanted the stayhole, only to be greeted with a stinging pussfull of flying particles of coal. There was a trick to this. The pick had to be aimed at the spot, and just before it struck the coal, I had to shut my eyes and duck my face. Even with eyes wide open, and face up, I could not hit the exact spot I aimed at. I really missed when I had to close my eyes and duck my head before the pick hit. I finally got the stayhole dug, but by the time I finished with the pick, my arms were like lead, and little specks of coal were stuck to my coal-dust-blackened, sweat-soaked face.

Then I sharpened a timber with the axe, so it would fit into the stayhole, and held it against the roof with my shoulder. While holding it there, I put the pan shovel and pick together, and in line with one another, held them under the unsupported end of the timber with the pan shovel on the pavement. Then I slid the pick along the shovel until the pick touched the timber. Then I let the strap fall. Holding the pick and pan shovel in that position, I laid them on another timber, and cut that timber the length measured by the pick and shovel. I then put the strap back into the stayhole and supported the other end of the strap with the timber measured for that purpose. I had to remember to take six more timber off the pan line when they came down.

All this would not be much for a seasoned loader,

but it was a lot of work for me. By the time I got the strap and timber up, I was getting more tired, and more worried. The shift was almost half over, but I was only one third finished. There were still six more holes to shoot, and load, and three more straps to put up. My legs were like rubber. I was not going to finish on time. Even though it made the shift longer, I was glad the pan line stopped thirteen or fourteen times for ten-minute intervals while they changed a full trip for an empty one. I could rest, and have a bite to eat.

I duffed under the next bottom hole, and shouted for the shotfirer. When he came this time, he offered me some kind advice. He said that one plug of powder would be enough for this hole. I said okay. The shotfirer was right. When the hole was fired, all the coal came down in nice-sized lumps. I loaded as fast as I could, getting more tired as the shift went on. The thick coal dust didn't make it any easier. Chewing tobacco kept me spitting dust out of my mouth, but it was a mixed blessing. Since I couldn't swallow any tobacco juice, my throat got very dry. Finally I said to hell with the chew, and simply ate dust.

I was shooting my last hole at home time. Not bad—even better, I wasn't the only one still loading. There were three or four others still not finished. This made me feel good—I wasn't as bad as I thought I might be. The eight-hour shift was over, but I was going to finish the section, and finish it I did! In nine hours I had loaded about eighteen tons of coal, and put up four straps. I was proud of myself, and quite satisfied. As I walked out the level for home, I was reaping my reward. Nobody loaded a section of coal and walked away feeling worthless. I was very tired, but I felt like a king! Even if nobody knew the "giants" killed that day, I did, and this knowledge carried a sense of worth with it. A satisfied grin became part of my character. I longed to tell someone, but the only ones who could understand this were other miners. That closed the society quite a bit.

# 7

# The Diesel

TUESDAY MORNING, and it was back to routine gob work. However, the routine was about to be broken by a very pleasant surprise.

I had just changed into my pit clothes for day shift when the underground manager came to me and said: "Stay on the surface today. They are going to show you how to run one of those diesels." Then he turned to talk to someone else about another matter. This came completely out of the blue. I had heard about the diesels, but never gave them any serious thought. As far as I was concerned, I would never be given anything to do with them. But someone in management thought I had potential, so I was given a chance at this new job.

Maybe it was because I was going to night school. Whatever, I was now desperate for more information. I asked around and found out that two diesel mine locomotives had arrived at 12 Colliery, and were now at the shop—a large building which was the mechanical heart of the colliery.

This news was so good that I was afraid to believe it. I held my enthusiasm in check—allowing for the possibility that this job was really for someone else, and the underground manager had told me by mistake. As the day went on, I joined three others who had also been chosen—two for each diesel—and together we began to learn the ropes. I couldn't wait to tell Norma about my good fortune, even though she could never understand.

Each diesel weighed fifteen tons, was about fifteen feet long and five feet high. They were driven by a 100-horsepower, five-cylinder engine, top r.p.m. (revolutions per minute) of 1250—not much more than idle speed for today's car engines. These first two diesels had three-speed transmissions. Top speed was fifteen and a half miles per hour on the flat, much slower up grade, and one hell of a lot faster on the downgrade. The pistons were five inches in diameter with a six-and-a-half-inch stroke. If this engine stalled, it was the operator's fault, not the engine's

Their only limitation was their traction. This fifteen-ton weight rode the rails on four wheels. Four points of contact—steel on steel. If the wheels didn't slip, these things could haul anything that was coupled to them.

On a downgrade, the operator was not supposed to let a full trip push the diesel faster than three and a half m.p.h. (miles per hour) in first gear, six and a half m.p.h. in second gear, or fifteen and a half m.p.h. in high gear. Other than that, throw the thing out of gear and use the Westinghouse air brake. Otherwise the full trip would make the engine rev over 1250 r.p.m. Good theory. In fact, in first or second gear, a full trip might make the engine rev slightly over 1250, but not much—the engine would simply drag the wheels. This thing proved to be one brute of an engine.

Me and my diesel operator buddies, much to our delight, were taken to several workshops—some in Sydney. It was really a treat for me to think that instead of being underground pounding on chuck blocks, I was going to Sydney to learn more details on diesel engines and the workings of the manual transmission. At these sessions, it was heavily impressed upon us that we were not to start the engine until we checked: (1) the engine oil; (2) the transmission oil; (3) the gearbox oil; (4) the two-stage air compressor oil; and (5) the fuel pump oil.

We also had to check the water in the radiator and the "conditioner" tank. The conditioner tank was a tank full of water through which the exhaust gasses passed. The water would extinguish any bits of burning carbon in the exhaust before it entered the mine air. The electrical system on the diesels also had to be approved for underground, and we had to keep it up to standards.

I was more than happy to comply with all the instructions. This stuff was very expensive, and needed to be operated properly. I was also much happier to do this than to shift pans or work in the gob. I didn't know it yet, but the danger on this new job was up more than a notch or two.

NORMA AND I HAD BEEN GOING TOGETHER for about two years, and I felt that it would be nice to spend the rest of my life with her. She must have felt the same, since she thought that getting married was a good idea. There was no big "pop the question" night—just a shared feeling that this was it for us. One day I simply said: "Let's get married." And Norma said: "Okay."

Both our families were very much coal mining families. We each lived about equal distance on either side of 18 Colliery. Norma's dad and younger brother worked in 18 Colliery, and her other brother worked in 12 Colliery. As a matter of fact, Bobby, the brother in 12 Colliery, came as close as it gets to getting killed. He got caught under a gob when it came in. The doctors gave up on him, but he made it. The only thing that saved his life was the duff under his head. Had it been solid stone, he would have been a goner for sure.

Economically, both Norma and I were brought up just under the "enough" line. We both knew what it was to do without. Limited finances set the priorities. We both went to work to help our families out. We both knew we would never be rich, but we didn't have to be. Life together was beautiful, and we looked forward to living it that way—together.

There was one thing the coal mining society imposed upon us to which we were totally oblivious. As a woman, Norma had no choice but to be the one who looked after the children and kept the house in order. I was expected to be the wage earner and, as father of any children we might have, I was also to be the authority figure. I was to be emotionally tough. Norma could cry if she felt like it. This gender role expectation was a sacred cow that was to bring grief to both of us. But there was one thing Norma and I both took from our immediate society and from our families— commitment! When a couple got married, that was it—for life!

AFTER A WEEK OR SO TRAINING for diesel operator, I went back to routine gob work with Frank, and waited for the day when they would start using the diesels in the mines. The day came soon enough—just as unexpected as the original announcement that I was to be trained.

## The Diesel

It was another day shift Monday, and there was no work in the gob section, so I went looking for another shift. I thought: "If I am going to work that hard carrying timber, I might as well go for another section of coal—at least the pay will be better." With more confidence this time, I approached the 19 West production overman and asked for a section of coal. As I feared—but not so much this time—I got again what I asked for. I went for a can of powder and an early rake. I would need all the time I could get.

When I got down to the section, my panic was not as bad this time, but it was still there. I planned the duffing of the section, but I never got the chance to break into a sweat. Barely had I started to look under the pans for a spot to get the duffing shovel through, when an old school chum appeared at the section.

"Hey, Jack, you got a section here too?"

Jack said: "Yes, this one. They want you in 19 East to run the diesel!"

Once again, I was almost afraid to believe what I was hearing. Jack told me they had already taken a diesel down and they were ready to see if it would fit in and out 19 East Level. Jack took my section, and I left immediately for 19 East to get the diesel ready for the coal shift tomorrow. I left Jack to load the section of coal.

Upon arriving at 19 East, I found the diesel already running. The mechanic had started it. The underground manager was there, and other officials, plus some troubleshooters in case anything had to be moved. They were ready to take the diesel in the level. I was told to get at the controls and start in slowly. This first trip in the level was memorable.

The road was good in 19 East, and the arch rails

were still arched—hardly bent at all, because this was a new level. This cautious trial run was because the diesel was a foot or so higher than the boxes. Everyone knew the boxes would fit, no problem, because they had been used since the wall and level began. However, the extra height of the diesel was in question. Obviously, it would not hit the roof, but what about the low side of the arch rails? The road was not in the middle of the level, but to the low side. If there was any problem, everyone expected it would be the top left side of the diesel hitting the left, low side of the arch rails. That's where everyone was watching, and as far as anyone could see—no problem—lots of room between the diesel and the arch rails.

But about halfway in the level—POW!—like an explosion, but not like an explosion, because the POW did not let up. Even though the lights of those around were no more than three feet away, nothing could be seen because of the thick dust. It was panic and pandemonium.

But not for long. It only took a few seconds after the initial blast before everyone knew what had happened. The *low side* corner of the diesel—where no one was watching—had hit a coupling on the eight-inch air line, and had torn it off. Now, 100 pounds per square inch of compressed air roared continuously from the low side. As soon as I could see a few feet behind, I reversed the diesel and went back out the level to shut the air off at the main valve on the landing.

I hardly got back in when the coupling was repaired. The guys on hand for just that sort of thing made short work of it. I went back out to turn the air on again, and everything was back to normal. But a lesson had been learned. The boxes could pass this coupling because they were rounded at their bottom corners. The diesel was not. It needed four to six inches more room at its bottom corners. Consequently, the road had to be jacked out from the eight-inch air line, here and at several other places.

After this mishap, one guy walked ahead of the diesel, checking the room between it and the couplings. His eye prevented further surprises. It took a while, but once inside at the spare road, management was satisfied that the diesel could now move in and out the level at speeds for which it was designed. And what it was designed for was waiting on the spare road: there, waiting for *its* trial run, was a full trip.

I felt the adrenaline shoot into my stomach. During the training period on the surface, I had coupled up to four or five boxes full of timber. The diesel moved these around like trinkets, and stopped them on the proverbial dime. Now, however, I coupled the diesel to sixteen boxes—all completely full of coal. No trinkets here—this was the real thing. The combined weight of the diesel, boxes and coal would be about seventy-five tons, and it felt like it.

I shifted into reverse, and slipped the gear selector into first gear. I could feel the diesel taking the weight of each box as it pulled at the couplings. The engine still idled, but it was a more serious, work-sounding idle now as it took the weight of the whole trip.

Now open the throttle and go to top speed in first gear. Close the throttle again and shift into second gear. I was on the way out the level with my first full trip.

Top speed in second gear was as fast as I was willing to go until I found out just how long it would take to stop this thing. No way was I waiting until I *had* to stop. Officials on the trip or not, I threw the transmission out of gear and applied the Westinghouse air brake. The boxes all bumped up to the diesel, but as far as slowing down was concerned, precious little was happening. In fact, for an instant, I wondered if the brakes were working at all. I panicked a bit, and applied more air pressure to the brake—too much more! The wheels stopped turning and slid along the rails like skis, making a frying sound.

With the wheels stopped, it felt like the diesel and full trip actually increased in speed. For sure, the diesel lost all braking power when the wheels stopped. I released the air brake and the wheels started turning again. The trip, however, did slow down slightly.

I put the transmission back into second gear and brought the diesel and trip back up to second-gear speed. There was still a lot of level left before the trip had to be stopped, so I took another try at stopping.

I put the transmission back in neutral and applied the air brake again—this time with a cooler head. The boxes bumped up, jolting the diesel and driving it out the level like a cork in a stream. But this was only a short-lived response. The brakes quickly took over, and I could feel that the whole trip was indeed under control. This thing was not going to stop suddenly, but it was definitely going to stop, and I could pretty well guess the distance it would take. That's what I wanted!

I still didn't shift into third gear, however. That would come with practice. Just get the thing safely stopped on the landing for now. Tomorrow was another day, and the officials would not be so numerous or attentive. As for now, when it came time to stop, the trip behaved pretty much as I thought it would. As a matter of fact, I had to pull the trip out a bit to where it was supposed to stop. I had been overly cautious. That was soon to change.

The first shift on the diesel was over, and what a pleasant change! No longer did I have to spend most of the day crawling around on all fours. Now I could stand erect when I felt like it. As a matter of fact, I didn't even have to stand—I had to sit down to operate the diesel. From the cramped wall in the gob, to the spacious level on the diesel, was quite a switch, right down to my pit clothes.

With the exception of socks and shorts, which I changed, on average, once a week, pit clothes would remain in the wash house from one vacation time to the next—a year. Those of us working on the wall would get these clothes very dirty, dusty, and sweaty. When each shift was over, and we were in the wash house ready to shower, we would take them off, hang them on hooks, raise them close to the rafters in the wash house and, after showering, change into our street clothes. That meant that our dusty, sweaty pit clothes hung in the hot wash house overnight, or for the weekend, awaiting the start of the next shift.

It was extremely uncomfortable putting these pit clothes back on again, since now they were very dry, and actually hard where the sweat dried on them—not to mention the aroma—especially the socks. The dust, too, was dustier, because now it was a dry dust. A lot of guys would beat their clothes against the wall or on the bench to smooth them a bit and knock some dust from them. Even then, pulling a sweat shirt on over your head was enough to streak your face with the coal dust from last shift. I simply dressed in my pit clothes as they were. After moving around in them for a few minutes, they started to break in again, and by the time I was on the rake ready to go down, the pit clothes felt as good as they ever did.

Now, as a diesel driver, my pit clothes were not so dirty, dusty, or sweaty—not even the socks. Instead of dust and sweat, they smelled of diesel fuel and diesel exhaust. Oil now instead of dust. Putting the pit clothes on now at the start of the shift was almost the same as putting my street clothes on at the end of the shift. It was, however, still the "pit."

Miners were a close and friendly group, but on the rake, they were *literally* close. Each miner was seated with his knees up in about a two-foot space. It was not uncommon for the guy in front to use the knees of the guy behind him as a back rest. Consequently, the rake ride down was not exactly a lesson in etiquette or good manners. This was the pit, and just about anything goes. If a guy felt like blowing a fart, he did, and while those of us upwind of him complained, and may have felt like throwing up, we knew we could do the same.

Again: there was to be no smoking or open flame in the coal mine, so ninety-nine percent of us chewed tobacco. Word had it that this was to keep us from swallowing too much dust, since the tobacco kept us spitting. Closer to the truth, however, was the fact that it satisfied our craving for nicotine. Most guys, as soon as they were on the rake, put in a chew. It was not unusual, once the rake started moving, for one guy to eject a streak of tobacco juice, and others above him to feel the spray in their faces. Sometimes I could tell what kind of tobacco a guy was chewing.

The words of the song "Squid Jigging Grounds" come to mind: "If you get cranky without your silk hankie..."—stay home! The coal mine was a dirty, messy place. I can't ever remember seeing a coal miner use a "hanky" to blow his nose. When you blow your nose in the coal mine, close your right nostril with your right thumb, bend over a bit, and blow like hell! Do the same for the left nostril. Personally, I would not want to be seen using a hanky underground.

The same "creature comforts" went for bathroom procedures. Once underground, you simply turned your back and let 'er go for number one. A little more consideration was expected for number two. You were expected to go a little off the beaten path for that—into a cutoff along the level, or back into the gob as far as you dare go safely. When you did go for number two, don't bother looking for a nice clean, white porcelain toilet bowl with the seat down. There were no such things, nor were there rolls of nice, soft toilet paper conveniently placed. If you had time to look for an old stone dust bag, that is the best you could expect. Stone dust bags were made of layered, rough brown paper. What you did was to tear off the inside layer with the stone dust on it, and use the other layers—not very tender! And when you saw little pieces of stone dust bag, step carefully and take small breaths!

Level dirt was different from wall dirt. The wall had more clutter, and it could take about ten minutes to travel up a 500-foot wall due to the clutter and tight places. But the wall was always changing—moving toward the ever-moving coal face. As the coal was mined, all the machinery and roof supports had to be moved to the new face.

Not so with the level. Aside from its closing in slowly, it remained the same. Consequently, the dirt remained the same, or piled up. The "pigeon holes," where the landing tenders stayed, were generously sprayed with months of stale tobacco juice. When it got so bad the landing tenders themselves couldn't stand it, it could not be removed. The only remedy was to cover it with stone dust, which did little for the smell, and not much for the sow bugs that crawled around in the damp stuff. If this were the wall, this spot would be changed to a new one every second day, but on the level, this was it—year in and year out, until the wall was finished.

The rats, too, were constant visitors, more so than on the wall, especially if there was a crust of bread or the smell of a lunch can close by. A lot of miners, even when they had the chance, would not sleep in the pit, afraid a rat would run over them—a legitimate fear. Some guys would sleep, but only after tying their pants around their ankles so the rats could not run up their pant legs. It was not uncommon to hear rodent squeals from the rats as they fought, or whatever, then see one running away from the scene. Trying to spit tobacco juice on a running rat was a favourite pastime.

A common smell was that of a dead rat that had been run over by a trip. Sometimes they would only be maimed, and have enough strength to get in the rib behind some timber and die where no one could find them. Bad enough removing a dead rat from a place of work when it could be seen, but to look for one was even worse. As a matter of fact, two greasy, oily, very dead rats greeted me from the bottom of the grease pit on my second shift in 19 East. No smell yet, but they would have to be removed. Hopefully the maintenance guy would do it. If not, once they started to stink, the first guy who had to spend some time around the grease pit would move the rats for sure.

The smell of diesel smoke was a new aroma in the coal mine. When the diesel engine was first started, and the engine was cool, I actually liked the smell of the exhaust, especially after it was filtered through the fresh water in the conditioner tank. However, once the diesel had hauled a trip or two, and had over-heated, it was a different matter. The exhaust then was thick and black, with nothing pleasant about it at all. It was just plain stinky!

I COULDN'T WAIT TO GET STARTED on my second shift on the diesel, but I would have to wait, because the diesel engine was not as anxious as I was to get started. As a matter of fact, it would not start at all! There were two tanks on the diesel, each filled with 450 pounds per square inch of compressed air. This air pressure is what rolled the diesel engine over to start it. This worked just fine when the engine was warm. This morning, however, the engine was cold—too cold to start. I opened the valve to the first tank, sending air to the distributor, then jabbed the starter, and lis-tened to the engine turning over. It sounded like tur-nips rolling down carpeted stairs.

Soon—too soon—all the compressed air was used. The engine did not start, and I suspected that it was not going to start. I closed that valve, opened the one to the second tank, and jabbed the starter again. Same result—no start! The thing was dead in the wa-ter. The only hope now was an auxiliary tank and compressor unit on a tram in behind the diesel on the same tracks. I started the electric-motor-driven com-pressor, and waited until the pressure in the auxiliary tank reached 450 p.s.i. Then I hooked the hose to the diesel and tried again to start the engine. No go!

Now I started to sweat it. This thing was not going to be started by the time the last rake arrived with the men. They would not be pleased if they had to walk in. In a last-ditch effort, I left the auxiliary tank hose connected to the diesel, opened the valves of all three tanks, and started the auxiliary compressor again. I planned to wait until it filled all three tanks to 450 p.s.i., then give it all three at once. It wouldn't turn over faster, but it would turn over longer. It might or might not do the trick—but I never got the chance to find out.

Before the tanks were filled, the mechanic arrived. He said: "No, we only need one tank," and he shut two of them off. The mechanic had known this would probably happen, so he came prepared. He leaned toward me and said in a hushed voice: "For christ' sake, b'y, don't tell anyone I got this." He took a small bottle from his inside jacket pocket. It was filled with naphtha gas—highly illegal in a coal mine.

He waited until the one tank was just about filled to 450 p.s.i., took the intake air filter off, splashed some naphtha inside the intake passage, put the filter back on, and jabbed the starter. It started, but with one hell of a rattle and banging. It sounded like automatic small arms fire—like every piston blew its cylinder head. I thought we had wrecked the engine. As a matter of fact, it didn't hurt the engine at all. While it billowed an unbelievable amount of white smoke, it quickly settled down to its normal, rumbling idle, and stopped making so much smoke.

Now we waited a bit for the engine to warm up before putting it to work.

## The Diesel

The naphtha trick turned out to be a "blind eye" decision by management. It had to be. That was the only way these cold diesel engines would start—especially after standing for the weekend. For now, this was the only diesel in the pit, so it was just me, the other operator, and the mechanic who used naphtha. Anyone who asked management if they could take a bottle of naphtha down, the answer would be a definite "NO!" So nobody asked. But from now on, the engine always started.

The shift was now ready to begin, albeit with a pissed-off crew because they had to walk in. The diesel was supposed to drive them in, but I could not get it going in time. Now, it was going, and I moved the diesel out of the "stable," coupled it to an empty trip, and started pushing that in. That was another "blind eye" decision by management. The trip was supposed to be pulled in, not pushed, but for now this was not possible.

Once on the spare road, the endless haulage positioned the trip under the chute and loading was about to begin. The endless haulage was simply a steel rope, like a clothesline on pulleys, set between the road rails. As one side of the rope moved in, the other side moved out. Just hook the trip onto the rope of choice with a vice-like grab. While that trip was being loaded, I went out for another one, pushed it in, and parked it on the "empty" road of the spare road. It wasn't long before the first trip was loaded, and put on the "full" road.

Now, thought I, we are in business. All the officials were up the wall watching the performance of another newcomer to the mine—a machine that management called the Dosco Miner, and the workers called "The Pig." While they were away, I would find out just what the diesel could do.

I coupled to the full trip, and started out. No "second gear only" this time. I went through first, second, then slipped the transmission into third. Third gear had the speed of the other two gears combined. The transmission sounded a low-pitched moan which rose as the throttle was opened—like a gas tank filling up. I could feel the wind as the speed increased, but I was still cautious. I would not open the thing all the way. This was only my second trip.

I went just under full speed, and tried stopping the full trip again. I threw the transmission out of gear, and applied the air brake. The initial jolt, and the feel of being carried along like a cork in a stream, was there—but I waited, and sure enough, the diesel started to slow the trip down. No problem. It was obvious that the trip could not be stopped quickly, but once the stopping distance of the diesel and full trip were calculated, enough distance from where the brakes were first applied could be set aside for a full stop.

I was ready to open this thing out all the way, so I brought the next full trip out most of the way at top speed. The diesel dipped and heaved as it went over low rail joints, its springs cushioning the bumps, and the arch rails, scarcely a foot away, whizzed by in a blur, giving the impression of a speed well over fifteen miles per hour. Caution still ruled. I cut power and applied the brakes before I really had to. But that was short-lived.

There were about fifteen trips to a shift. Before this shift was over, I had a spot marked on the level— a certain twisted arch rail. If I had sixteen full boxes on, cut power, and applied the brakes at that rail, I could easily stop the trip where it had to be stopped.

Hauling coal began in earnest. I was still cautious, but only about getting the full trip stopped where it was supposed to stop. As far as stopping anywhere along the level—forget it. The full trip was in command—get out of the way! And that's what anyone did who happened to be on the level when the diesel was coming.

Towards the end of every shift, a pair of brushers would be walking in the level to get an early start on their work. When they saw the diesel coming, they would get as far to the high side as possible, and cringe against the rib. Although the speed of the diesel was not excessive for the 19 East rails, they were not used to seeing trips go that fast. One of them was so uneasy that he made a bet with his buddy that within a month I would be taken up in blotters, because the diesel would surely jump the road, and the full trip and arch rails would turn me into a grease spot. Happily, he lost his bet.

IT WAS NOT A VERY BIG WEDDING, because we could not afford it. Norma and I got married on July 31, 1954—July 31, because two weeks miners' vacation started on August 1. We had saved and planned. The first honeymoon night had to be secret, or there would have been none of the privacy we both wanted. We were the only two who knew we would spend the first night at Sydney River Cabins, just fifteen miles from home.

The ceremony was simple but sincere. After our vows, and during the singing, I offered a prayer: "God, please kill me before I live long enough to break these vows." That prayer was misdirected, since God does not kill people, but my commitment was not misdirected: I knew I would never do this again. Nor, I thought, would Norma. This was as pure as it gets.

I had a good job now, and a good woman. My love life changed for the better. However, my underground life was about to change for the worse.

# 8

# 17 West

**M**Y DAYS IN 19 EAST came to a sudden end. Part of my job was to go down early and get everything ready to drive the men in. On what I thought was just another regular day in 19 East, I was ready and waiting for the men to get into the empty trip and start in. But I would not be taking them in. The overman came down with a replacement diesel runner, and told me I was to go to 17 West. They had just started using another Dosco Miner to cut coal on that wall, and wanted a diesel on the haulage level. I was to operate this diesel. The danger went up another notch.

The haulage level here was what was called the "slant." It was a branch off the main level—something like a "Y." It angled away from the main level for about 400 feet, then it went parallel with the main level. This slant was at the bottom of 17 West, and the main level was at the top.

This time, I walked in the bottom slant level. The shift had already started, so the diesel was inside waiting for the first trip to be loaded. There was another guy on it, but they were sending him up the wall to run the Dosco Miner. I was to ride with him for a few trips to get used to the level.

The wild card part of it was the slant—it was

quite steep where it joined the main level. Word had it that you had better not get caught going too slow coming out of the slant, or the diesel would not pull the full trip up the grade, and would go back in by the run. What I had to find out was just where to "give 'er the beans" to get up the slant.

In an underground tunnel, or level, everything looks the same. A new guy could not tell just where the slant was. What I needed was a mark to tell me I was about to climb the grade and go around the turn. It was something like 19 East. I had a mark there where I cut power and applied the brake. Here I needed a mark that would signal when to set the speed of the diesel so that it would be going fast enough to climb the grade, but not too fast to go around the curve.

Two trips with the guy were all that I got, then he went up the wall and left me on my own. Two trips were not enough. I could not remember just where the slant started. To make matters worse, there was a crew of road makers at the top of the slant bracing the rails. This was so that the fifteen-ton diesel would not turn out a rail and go straight into the rib instead of around the curve. These guys did not want any surprises. Unfortunately, they were about to get one.

On the way out with my first full trip, I did not know exactly where I was at any given time. I cursed my own stupidity for not jamming a stone dust bag or something behind the rails at the bottom of the slant when I walked in. Now it was too late. I would get hell if I stopped the trip about halfway out and started walking to see where the slant was—that would take too much time. Stopping the trip closer to where I thought the slant was would also be out of the question—maybe I would not be able to get going fast enough from a full stop if I had to start again too close to the grade. All I could do now was guess: this must be about a quarter of the way out—now about halfway—the slant can't be far now. The last thing I wanted was to get stuck on the slant and have the trip go back in by the run. I convinced myself that I had been going long enough, the slant must be close, and I had better get this thing moving.

I shifted into high gear and opened the throttle. The usual low-pitched moan came from the transmission, and it started to get higher as speed increased. I was expecting the upgrade to begin any second now, but it did not. My expectation remained the same, but the speed did not—it was increasing. Surely the slant grade would start in the next few feet—but no grade yet! Fact is: I left the throttle open too long. I was now at top speed—the transmission sounding a high-pitched whine and the arch rails whizzing by in a blur. No problem for going up the grade, but definitely too fast for the curve. I closed the throttle again, but too late. The boxes barely bumped up to the diesel when there it was—the slant! I thought of Norma. This could be the end of us.

There was no hope of slowing down now, and I did not want the brakes on going around the curve. My only option was to open the throttle again to overcome some of the lateral force the diesel was going to exert on the outside rail of the curve. I did just that. The front of the diesel pointed upwards, and it felt like an airplane just starting its takeoff. I went around the curve like the proverbial "shit through a tin horn."

I felt, and was extremely thankful for, the expertise of the road makers. The outside rail on the curve actually felt like it was pushing me away from the high side rib, and safely onto the main level rails. They had the road banked and the rail braced perfectly. It was a dangerous and exciting experience, but thankfully, it only lasted three or four seconds, and there was no pile-up. More: I was still alive and well—and so were all the road makers!

The road makers were caught by surprise. They had heard the diesel coming, but did not expect to have it appear so suddenly. Their lamps looked like a swarm of startled fireflies all going one way—into the main level away from the curve. They thought the diesel was going to jump the road and bring the place in on top of them. I thought the brusher in 19 East would win his "grease spot" bet.

But the road makers had the rail braced well enough so that it held. The diesel and full trip went safely around the curve and switched to the main level. On the way back in, the road makers' lamps were all pointed at me, and they were shouting. Because of the noise of the engine and empty boxes, I could not hear what they were saying. But I didn't have to hear—I could guess. For sure, it was the same language I used on Sawdust to get him to move out of the gundy hole, and if my arse had been close enough to them, it would have been well kicked.

As routine took over, and I got to know the level, I found that the steepness of the slant grade had been overstated. The grade was steep, but short. By the time that shift was over, I knew where the slant started, and how much speed was needed to get up the grade. The diesel and first few boxes could mount the grade and safely switch to the main level at about half speed in third gear. Then it would slow down quickly, since the rest of the trip was still on the grade. A simple down shift into second gear at wide open throttle pulled the rest of the trip nicely over the grade and on the way out the main level.

Learning experience grew with the days in 17 West. The slant was *mostly* flat—no grades to deal with other than this one where the slant joined the main level. The main level, however, was a different story. From the slant out, it was not really steep, but steep enough for caution. I no longer had the option of picking a spot where I could cut power and apply the brakes. No power at all was needed, and the brakes had to be on *all* the time. The full trip had to be under constant control. If it picked up too much speed, it could not be stopped at the landing. Luckily, the landing was relatively flat. The same could not be said for the main level *inside* the slant. This was a very dangerous part of running diesel in 17 West.

While the coal was being taken off the wall and hauled out the slant level, the maintenance shift was busy in the main level at the top of the wall. The level here had to be "brushed"—that is, kept open enough for boxes and trams full of material to get in to the top of the wall. For this purpose, they had an "emco" machine. It loaded boxes with stone. Once loaded, a "tugger"—a mini hoist—put the boxes, one at a time, on a small siding. Why in hell they ever picked the spot they did for this siding, I never knew. It was more of a cliff than a grade. At the inside of this siding, they had a short piece of steel rope anchored to an arch rail. As each box was loaded with stone, it was lowered out the level and pulled back in on this siding. Like out one arm of a "Y" and back in the other. Then it was coupled to this anchored rope. Six boxes were all they could put on this siding—thank heavens!

The "pain in the ass" part of this was that after the coal shift was over, I could not go home. I had to go back in and get these boxes. The dangerous part of it was that the diesel had all it could do to push these boxes in enough so that someone could pull the pin and uncouple them from the rope anchor. It was not unusual for me to try four or five times to push these boxes in *one inch* so that the pin could be pulled. Once the pin was pulled, look out! The diesel and boxes were on their way out. This particular grade was very steep, but it was also short. Still, a cool head had to prevail, especially if the diesel happened to be one of the new automatic transmission diesels.

Once these automatic transmission diesels had applied full power to the gearbox to push the boxes in, and the pin was pulled to let the boxes go, the diesel gearbox could not be immediately reversed. A few seconds were needed for the engine to return to complete idle and the oil pressure to leave the gearbox. During this time, the diesel and boxes of stone started out. This is where the cool head was needed. The operator had to lock the wheels with the air brake, wait three or four seconds even though the diesel was sliding out, *then* shift into reverse. Once in reverse, he would let the brake off until the wheels started turning again, then get control over the trip before it got to the next downgrade.

If the operator tried to shift into reverse immediately, with the wheels turning, the gear selector would get caught between forward and reverse, and the diesel and boxes would roller coaster off the grade. It needed sand to the wheels in order to keep the trip under control, but the sander valve was connected to the forward/reverse gear selector. In order to have sand for reverse travel, the gearbox had to be all the way into reverse. And without sand, the chances of keeping the trip under control were very slim.

Whoever the diesel driver was, he had to know all this and be prepared before he gave the slack so the boxes could be unhooked from the rope anchor. One experienced operator was sent in on a maintenance shift to leave some empty boxes and take out the full ones—but it was his very first time in this particular place. He was unaware of the ride these few boxes would give him once they were unhooked from the rope. After leaving the empties, he coupled to the full ones, got them bumped in enough to get the pin pulled, then had the ride of his life.

Too quickly, he tried to shift into reverse. No go! The selector got caught between forward and reverse. Like it or not, he was in neutral—and so were the sanders! Without sand, he was unable to get the trip under control before it started down the next grade. Once on the way down the second grade, he knew there was no hope of getting the thing under control again, so he jumped off and let it go. He became a near fatality when his lamp cord got caught on the Westinghouse air brake. Had it not broken immediately, it would have dragged him under the wheels.

The diesel and trip went down the grade at breakneck speed until they spread the rails and dropped between them, tearing up 200 feet or more of road before finally plowing to a stop. It took a small army of road makers a full shift to repair the road and get the diesel and boxes back on the rails. After this happened, the mechanics took the automatic transmission diesels, disconnected the sander valve from the forward/

reverse selector, and tied it into the reverse position.

I gained a lot of experience on the 17 West main level grades. I was going to need it all—and more. I had just got the nod that I was to start hauling coal out of 16½ East. The danger went up another notch.

NORMA AND I STAYED with my parents for a while after we were married, but that didn't work. We joked that we were spending too much money on the kleenex we stuffed in the bedsprings to keep them quiet. A month or so was enough.

Try as we might, we could not get the backing we needed to buy the other end of the company house where Norma's parents lived. However, we could get a home improvement loan of five hundred dollars. That was enough to act on an idea Norma's dad had. He suggested that we fix up the old Sunday School building and live in that. He had made it into a garage, but with our own labour we could easily convert it to a two-room dwelling: kitchen and bedroom. That is what we did—with much pleasure!

Nothing was straight or tight, but it was home. Beautiful! I got a piece of eight-inch steel pipe from the pit for a chimney. Then we bought a new kitchen coal stove. The place was not insulated, but when that stove got going, none was needed—those two rooms were *too* hot. Boiled eggs for breakfast had to be put on spoons. If not, they would roll off the table. More than one winter morning Norma and I would wake up to a shovelful of snow on the foot of our bed. It blew in through a loose-fitting window. All these apparent inconveniences were actually fun. The adventure of being together in our very own home was pure joy. That was soon to change.

# 9

# The Half

EACH TIME I thought of The Half, it was another shot of adrenaline to the stomach, and for good reason. This was one of the older levels, driven for a "drop out donkey," which meant it was gravity that propelled the full trip out this level and, rest assured, the level was graded accordingly.

Not only that, the rails were not laid with a fifteen-ton diesel in mind. It wasn't until they began thinking about mechanization that they laid heavier rails. Consequently, about one half mile of the outside of this level was laid with light rails—ones that a fifteen-ton diesel locomotive could possibly turn over.

Adding to the problem was that the level was closing in. The diesel was going to be a very tight fit in here, and where it did miss the arch rails, many of them would be only inches away—space that could easily be closed by a speeding diesel dipping into a bad joint on the road. However, management was determined to haul coal out of The Half with a diesel.

The day came for the trial run. One bright spot: it was a brand-new diesel. The mechanic was there in case of bugs in the new machine. Compared to the old ones, this one rode like a Lincoln. The underground manager was there, and a few troubleshooters. They would earn their pay this day.

As we started in with the empty diesel, my worst fears were realized. The landing where we started was nice and wide, but once in the level a trip length or so, the place started to close in. Looking ahead as far as I could see, I was sure the diesel was not going to fit. With the underground manager behind me, kneeling on the bumper of the diesel, I inched my way in. Indeed, the diesel did not fit. Some of the arch rails touched the top of the diesel and dug in the whole length of it. These rails were marked for removal, but for now, we continued at a snail's pace on the way in.

Where the diesel passed the arch rails, it was so close that I could not poke my head above the instrument panel to check on more rails ahead. One of the guys there for troubleshooting went ahead on foot and watched to see how much clearance there was. I would lean out to the high side of the diesel and watch for his signals.

In more than one spot someone had to put a shovel between the front top left corner of the diesel and an arch rail, using the shovel as a shoehorn to slide past the rail, while I gingerly prodded the diesel ahead. This rail would have to be removed, and there would be hell to pay if we forgot it on the way out. The objective now was to get the diesel all the way in and see just how many arch rails had to be yanked out.

When we came to a rail that could not be passed, the troubleshooters tied a steel cable to it, and hooked the other end of the cable to the diesel. Then I reversed the diesel, took up the slack rope, applied sand to the rails, and then opened the throttle. Usually, the rail came out, but sometimes a good yank on the rope was necessary. However, the diesel always won. A sad note about this operation was that another diesel operator lost his life in this same procedure, getting his head caught in the limited space between the diesel and the arch rails.

It was a long shift, but by jacking the road away from the eight-inch air line and close rails, and by removing the arch rails that were in the way, we finally got the diesel all the way in. There were places on the level where there was enough room, but the tight places took a long time to get through. The next day was going to be more serious. Coal had to come out of this place, and this diesel had to haul it out.

THE UNDERGROUND MANAGER was there again the next day—a very watchful eye. The first order of business was to push an empty trip in. It was supposed to be pulled in with the headlight of the diesel announcing its location at all times; but for now, we had to find out if this arrangement with a diesel in The Half was going to work at all. I coupled to the empty trip, and with the underground manager with me again, started pushing the trip in.

Not long after starting on the diesel, I had been issued a special pit lamp. Only miners working around trips were allowed these lamps. They had highly polished reflectors, and when the bulb was adjusted to a focal spot, these things could light up objects at quite a distance. They were especially effective for men working around trips. The boxes were aluminum, and when these lamps shone on the boxes, they could be seen at a distance of a hundred yards or more. However, don't shine them in someone's eyes!

I continued in with the empty trip, this lamp focused on the boxes in front of the diesel—fifteen of them. When we started in, I could see them all, clear to the front end of the trip. After going about three to four hundred feet, however, the diesel started to slow down and labour. I thought the front boxes had jumped the road, but I quickly saw the problem. Although my lamp would easily show the whole fifteen boxes, all I could see were six boxes! I really did not want to believe what I was seeing. The boxes had disappeared into what seemed like a hole in the roof! They had gone *up* a steep grade and out of sight. Now I really worried. I had to come down this grade with fifteen *full* ones. Geez!

That was the worst grade, but there were more. That grade, although very steep, was relatively short. Once over that grade, the diesel still laboured, and was unable to shift into high gear. It was obvious that the boxes were still being pushed upgrade. The rest of the grades were gradual, but the level was uncomfortably steep for about the first half mile of the way in. Then, thankfully, it flattened out. Cautiously, we pushed the first diesel-powered empty trip all the way in to the spare road, and parked it there.

But now the scary part! The full trip was waiting. The adrenaline started flowing again. I felt threatened just by seeing it parked there—shiny aluminum boxes with black pillows of coal mounded high on them. The chute runner was always encouraged to get as much coal as possible in each box. He did. It was a point of pride for him. It made a chute runner's day to be told by an overman that his boxes were "beautifully loaded." As I eyed the "beautifully loaded" boxes, however, I wasn't proud. I was damn well scared.

Usually, I was more than ready to obey any order given by management. But when it came to this full trip, I got a bit political. I was not going to ask the underground manager if I could please take only half this trip at a time—I was going to tell him. No way was I hooking onto that thing and starting down those grades. A couple of practice runs were definitely in order, and I was going to have them. However, I never got the chance to inform the underground manager of my decision.

As I switched to the high road to couple to the full trip, the underground manager said: "Just take half this trip and come in empty for the other half."

I nodded my head in relieved agreement, and moved the diesel slowly towards the first box. One of the guys lifted the figure "8" club link on the box so that it entered the middle one of five slots in the front bumper of the diesel. The diesel bumped the box and the guy dropped the three-foot, two-inch-diameter pin through the link. The diesel was now coupled to the full trip. I shifted into reverse. Above the noise of the engine, I shouted to the guy: "Take seven," then started out slowly. The guy counted off seven full boxes, waved me "holt" with a right-left motion of his light, pulled the pin that connected the seventh to the eighth box, then with an up-and-down movement of his light, waved me out.

I wasn't scared now, but I was definitely excited. This was to be an information trip. The first half mile on the way out was great—good road, flat level, and reasonably roomy—so I let the automatic transmission shift into high gear and reach top speed. Not for long because, like any new level, I did not know the exact spot where the down grades started. I went for what I thought was long enough at top speed, then slowed to half speed and watched for the beginning of the down grades. It wasn't hard to see. The headlight of the diesel shone on the rails: two lines drawn out ahead of me. Soon the lines were erased—I could not see them. They disappeared below the beam of the headlight, and instead of rails and open level ahead, I could see only the roof of the level. I double-checked the air pressure for the brakes.

This was the spot, no doubt, and if I had not been able to see it, I could have felt it. As I started down the grades, I could actually feel the diesel tipping downward. I closed the throttle, reached for the Westinghouse air brake, and applied it slightly. I knew there would be spots where even just the seven boxes could not be stopped, but they definitely could be kept under control, and even if they did pick up some unwanted speed, there was a good, long, relatively flat spot just before the landing.

A runaway trip was not my concern this time. The concern now was to get the feel of the road, and a good idea of just how steep these grades were.

As I suspected, the grades called for respect and, unfortunately, so did the road—it was terrible. When I got to the grade I was so concerned about, the diesel tipped downward again, and the seven boxes weren't long making their weight felt. The diesel did pick up some unwanted speed, but nothing to worry about. Once on the flat road again, the half trip was easily brought back under control, and to a safe stop where it was supposed to stop.

I went back in empty for the remaining eight boxes, and hauled them out in a repeat and uneventful performance.

Practice was over. Now for the real thing!

I pushed another empty trip in. If the diesel could

complain, it surely would, because it laboured to push the empty boxes over the grades. As a matter of fact, it did complain a bit. The temperature gauge approached the boiling point of 212 degrees Fahrenheit, and it blew black smoke from the exhaust—just a forerunner of what was to come.

They were waiting for the empty trip when I got back in. Taking the full trip out in two parts took a lot of time, but it was time well spent as far as I was concerned. This first full trip was also going to take a lot of time. I would see to that. I was scared again, and I was going to keep as much control over this trip as possible. I switched to the high road, coupled to the full trip, and started out this time with the whole nine yards—fifteen "beautifully loaded" boxes of coal.

High gear and top speed as usual for the first half mile, but when I got to the spot where the grades started, I made sure that I was almost stopped. This was it—the stakes were really high now. Management was not at all sure the diesel locomotive could do the job here in The Half. Could it keep a full trip of fifteen boxes under control on these grades? I was the guy who had to find out for them. If I could not make this diesel hold the trip under control, someone could very easily get hurt—most likely me, since all hands who knew about this first trip were ready to dive for cover.

As soon as the diesel started to coast downgrade, I put on as much brake as I dared. The trick was to keep the wheels turning. Panic time if they stopped. It was something like a car on a very slippery road. A little bit of brakes gives some control, but lock up the wheels, and the car actually goes faster. As the boxes followed the diesel down the grade, they pushed it faster and faster—fast enough to make me very nervous—but I knew the trip would be in control on the steepest parts. I had to fight for a cool enough head to let the thing go until it reached a less steep part of the level, then "pile the binders to 'er'" in order to get the thing slowed down enough for the last grade—the steepest one of all—the "launcher" grade, as I was soon to name it.

With much relief, I got the trip down the first part of the grades, and under control again—going a bit faster than I wanted, but still under control. When I came to the top of the launcher grade—the one I feared most—I was going faster than I would have liked, but there it was. Like it or not, the diesel made its final downward dip. The boxes, already tight against the diesel, tipped into the grade one by one and launched the diesel out the level.

My heart pounded faster. Forget trying to slow the thing down now—just keep as much control as possible without locking the wheels, and most of all: keep a cool head. There was flatter level coming—I would make my play there. That is exactly what I did.

Once on the relatively flat level again, I applied as much pressure to the brakes as I dared. In just a few seconds, the trip started to slow down. I could see the empty trip parked on the landing, the full road was empty, and this full trip was still slowing down. I had more than enough room to get stopped—the diesel was under full control with at least three trip lengths of distance to spare.

The first nervous, highly over-cautious full trip was over. Now I knew the diesel could hold the full trip. As time went on, and I hauled more and more trips out of The Half, that three trip lengths of spare distance would be well used up. But for now, I was very relieved to have made it with the first full trip. That answered an important question: "Will the diesel locomotive hold a trip back in 16½ East Level?" Answer: "Yes, it will."

Now for the next part of that question: "Will a diesel haul coal out of 16½ East Level?" The over-cautious approach would never do the job. If the diesel was to haul coal out of The Half, it had to haul it fast! The level was a mile long, at least, and a trip could be loaded in ten to fifteen minutes if everything went well. I had to get a full one out, and an empty one back in, within that time.

Thus began a learning experience that never really ended for me. The trick on this level was to get as much air pressure on the brakes as possible without stopping the wheels. This was complicated by bad joints in the road. The diesel wheels, as all railroad wheels, had a raised two-inch flange around their inside circumference. When the diesel came to a bad joint, it "dove" into it, making this flange grind hard against the rail, causing increased friction. If the brakes were already applied with enough pressure to almost stop the wheels, the increased friction caused by the flange grinding against the rail *would* stop the wheels. Consequently, the air brake had to be slightly released just before every bad joint. If not, the wheels would lock at each bad joint, giving the operator one hell of a ride, and if it happened to be in 16½ East, it would not stop where it should.

Bottom line: I had better know where the bad joints were.

Engineers on surface railroads don't have this concern. If they need to make an emergency stop, they simply put the brake in the emergency position, and automatic sensors do the rest, keeping as much brake pressure on the wheels as possible without locking them. For me and other underground diesel operators, this was totally manual, and a talent that had to be learned from experience—something I could feel. By the speed of the trip, the steepness of the grade, and the roughness of the road, I knew at any given instant how much pressure to use. The Westinghouse air brake was like a musical instrument. The operator had to learn how to play it.

Hauling coal out of The Half called for respect. Now, however, I had the diesel wide open in high gear at the start of the grades, and when the diesel tipped downward, I reached under the throttle body to the linkage, and pulled on it to gain an extra fifteen to twenty r.p.m. out of the engine. Then, since the sanders were wired in reverse, I slipped the gearbox into neutral and closed the throttle. Then it was just me and the Westinghouse.

I knew every bad joint in the road, and just how fast I should be going at the top of the last steep grade—and rest assured, I was going as fast as I could get away with. I had it down so fine that the diesel would stop where it should with only six feet or so to spare.

Then came the day I hauled the first "trip that never stopped." Usually, I was able to get the full trip out and the empty one in before the last empty trip was loaded and pulled to the spare road. But they were getting better and better production results cutting coal with the Dosco Miner. They were loading the trips faster. This day, I could see the full trip coming just inside the spare road as I arrived in with the fresh empty trip. I switched to the full road and went out just ahead of the oncoming full trip. I stopped the diesel on the outside end of the spare road and, since it was flat there, left the brake off.

When the full trip was getting close to the diesel, I waved the haulage operator "holt." The trip slowed down, but it did not stop, since it was still dragging the endless haulage rope. I took the grab off the still-moving full trip, put it on the empty trip, tightened the ingoing rope on it, and waved the haulage operator in. Then I ran to the still-moving full trip, and lifted the link on the front box so it went into the proper spot in the diesel bumper. When the trip bumped the diesel, the diesel started moving. I dropped the pin through the link, then ran to the front of the diesel, got on, opened the throttle, and started out. The full trip never stopped!—and it would not stop until it reached the landing.

No one saw this performance. If they had, they would have thought it was no big deal. But to me, it was. I had just kept up with wide-open production. The Dosco Miner crew were at their best, and so was I. We were a perfect match. We had answered the question: "Can a diesel haul coal out of 16 1/2 East?" The answer: "Yes, it can!"

THE DOSCO MINER'S FULL NAME was supposed to be the Dosco Continuous Miner, but that name never had a chance. The miners quickly baptized it The Pig.

When The Pig first started, it was plagued with a lot of mechanical problems—yards and yards of hydraulic hoses, and cutting teeth that never seemed to be set just right. Instead of one cut for each shift, the best it could manage at first was two or three cuts a week.

But once the bugs were worked out, it was an amazing machine. Mining interests from all over the world came to see how it operated. By the time it was installed in 16½ East in 12 Colliery, it had been fine-tuned. Where it once took a flesh-and-blood miner about eight hours to load a twenty-ton section of coal, The Pig could rip out the same section in less than five minutes! When that thing dug into coal, its brute ripping power turned solid coal into duff and dust.

The cutting gib was like seven giant chain saws side by side. If it had a fault, it was that it made the coal too small. What saved the day for The Pig was the fact that coal-powered generating plants pulverized the coal anyway, and blew it into the furnaces. Not much pulverizing was needed for coal mined by The Pig.

The Pig was approximately fifteen feet long, five feet wide, and four feet high, and weighed about ten tons. Two 75-horsepower motors powered the 500-pick cutting gib, and a 30-horsepower motor powered the two caterpillar tracks and all the hydraulics. The Pig dragged two power cables and a water hose behind it. The cables were plugged in to a 500-volt power supply on the level. There were four operating levers at the back end of The Pig—one for each "cat" track, one for the "sump," and one for lifting the gib into the coal.

At the start of the shift, The Pig was in its "stall," a room dug into the solid coal face the length and width of The Pig, and into which it was maneuvered so that the long coal face was now in front of it.

The operator would position The Pig so that the nose with the cutting teeth touched the bottom of the coal. Then, locked on its cat tracks, the gib sump was extended eighteen inches in under the coal. This was simply an hydraulic telescoping of the gib section of the machine. Once under the coal, the gib would be lifted up into the coal by four hydraulic jacks, the rotating picks hauling the coal back from the nose of the gib onto a cross conveyor that spewed the coal onto the conveyor belt that took the coal down along the wall. The gib and cross conveyor looked like a waterfall in a fast-moving river of coal.

Once The Pig dug into the coal, it was *total* dust. Water, treated with a compound, was sprayed viciously on the front of the gib, but it did little to help. The operator still could not see where his gib was. A buddy had to stand positioned off to the gob side of the gib, and signal with his light when the gib was at the proper height. The operator would then stop the cutting before he penetrated above the roof coal.

This is the way it went all the way down the wall: move on the cat tracks to the coal—sump out eighteen inches under the coal—gib up, cutting to the roof coal—sump in—gib down—then repeat the same operation about three hundred times per shift, all the while breathing in copious amounts of coal dust. In those days, breathing masks were not used. A lot of the guys who operated The Pig, and who worked behind it, are now dead, and the rest suffer from silicosis.

Men who worked behind The Pig had the hardest job and the least pay. The Pig left a lot of duff behind it. This had to be shoveled out of the way so it could be "fleeted" back up the wall—taken back up to the top of the wall to get ready for another downwall cut. The Pig only cut in one direction. It would have been bad enough if this were just ordinary, dry duff. But the constant spray of water soaked the duff, making it very heavy. The poor guys that had to shovel it—called "muckers"—earned their pay.

And men who timbered behind The Pig laboured in water and dust, too. When The Pig was going good, they had to keep up with it, hurriedly putting up timber and straps where the coal used to be. The only time they could stop was when the trip was loaded, and The Pig had to stop—or when The Pig broke down. It was no picnic.

If The Pig could have had a continuous supply of empty boxes, it could truly have been a "Continuous Miner." Fact is, however, every time it loaded fifteen boxes, it had to stop and wait until fifteen more could be positioned under the loading chute on the level below. It was not unusual for The Pig and crew to load fifteen boxes—forty-five tons—in ten minutes. The men on diesel haulage had to keep up to this pace—and we did!

A YEAR AFTER WE WERE MARRIED, Norma and I had our first baby. He was a boy. We both were prepared now to be parents. But it was not to be. Something was very wrong. The little guy cried continually. In my absolute gender-role stupidity, I expected Norma to keep the baby quiet while I got some sleep. But she could not quiet the baby and, with no sleep, I was wearing down. Worse, I was no support at all for Norma.

I was unaware of it, but the worst part of the coal-mining culture was taking its toll. This was no time for gender roles, but we were both cast into them. Norma was getting the worst of it. I actually expected my supper to be ready when I came home from work.

My stupidity was short-lived. It was soon obvious

that this crying was not the crying of a healthy baby. Our baby cried so much that I actually feared for Norma's control over herself. There was no let-up. The little guy cried until he was so tired he had to sleep. As soon as he awoke from a very short sleep, he started to cry again. We had taken him to the doctor already, but we went back again and again.

One day when I came home from work, there was no baby—Norma had to leave him in the hospital. Our hopes went up. Maybe now, he would get the care he needed. A few days later, however, the hospital called and said we had better come in to see our baby—he was dying. We did. We had the minister come and baptize the little guy. He died five short weeks after he was born.

I always respected Norma, but after these five weeks, my respect for her grew. No way was she going to fall short of what was expected of her. All I had to do was get to work and haul coal. She had tried to stop a dying baby from crying. I can't remember the coal I hauled, but I will never forget how Norma came through in such a difficult time. Her commitment easily survived my stupidity. We picked up the pieces, and continued on.

MECHANIZATION was becoming the word in the Cape Breton coal mines. More diesels were coming into the pit now—six or seven of them. Soon, every level would have one. This required more operators and mechanics. But the new operators and mechanics were not trained as carefully as the original ones. They were trained on the job, by the seat of their pants. It wasn't long before the diesels were regarded as just more pieces of mine machinery and treated as such. Mechanics gave way to maintenance workers who really didn't care about giving the diesels the special care they required. The simple procedure of brake adjustment was one of their duties. It wasn't long before I became a victim of their sloppy maintenance.

It was the first full trip of the sixteen or so for the shift. This first trip was usually a bit slower, since it took three or four trips to get the rails well sanded. As usual, I checked the air pressure for the brakes well before I came to the top of the grades. It was 120 p.s.i. It was supposed to be 60 p.s.i., but the reducing valve that reduced it from 450 p.s.i. to 60 p.s.i. never worked as it should. No problem, however, since it was much better to have too much pressure than not enough. Just don't apply as much to the brake!

As the diesel tipped down and started out the grades, I immediately sensed something wrong. There was lots of pressure, but the brakes were not responding as they should have. It seemed as if at least half of their drag was missing! The trip was picking up too much speed. I increased the pressure, but the trip was not responding—it was still picking up speed.

Panic time! The trip was getting close to the last grade—the launcher grade—and it was going much too fast. I pulled out all the stops now! I opened the high pressure tanks and let them feed 450 p.s.i. to the reducing valve and low pressure tanks, then held the sander down steady and put the Westinghouse on the "lump"—a position just before the emergency position, which applied full pressure but still allowed for manual control. Down the grade now. I was thankful the reducing valve was not working. If it had been, I would have been flying, and probably would have jumped off by then. There was an unbelievable 120 p.s.i. on the brakes. It would have been impossible to keep the wheels turning with this pressure if things had been working as they should.

Back on the flat now, and the diesel was slowing down, but not nearly enough. I decided that, if the last full trip was gone to the surface, I would stay with the thing. If it were still there, I was going to bail off. In very short order I would find out—here came the landing. With relief, I noticed that the full trip had gone up—I had an open road—so I stayed on! I thought of Norma again.

I applied every bit of the 120 p.s.i. to the brakes now for most of the way out, as well as continuous sand, but as I approached the landing it was obvious the trip was not going to stop anywhere near where it should have. This thing was going to go around the drift and up the deep. I worried about the curve of the drift, but these rails were always well braced, and I was slowing down a bit.

As I was passing the empty trip on the landing, something else was different. I noticed a strange, orange glow reflecting from the empty boxes. "What in hell is *that*?" I leaned over the low side a bit to have a look, and what I saw terrified me. This friggin' thing was on FIRE! Actual flames were coming from the low side! The flaming diesel went well past the mark and up the drift. I could see the main haulage road on the auxiliary deep. The diesel stopped and went back down the drift, again passing the mark on the way in, but no matter now—the trip's energy was spent. The only thing speeding now was my heart! As for the trip, nothing derailed, and the fire went out!

What happened was that the mechanic on the maintenance shift had not adjusted the brakes correctly. The low side shoes were okay, but the high side ones were loose. This meant that I took a full trip out with two low-side brake shoes only, instead of all four. Not only did they get red, they melted the grease on the side rod bushings and started it ablaze. The brake shoes themselves were curled at the edges from being pressed hard to the wheels while red hot. As I looked at them now, they were still crackling and smoking, but the fire extinguisher was not needed.

What a ride! No one was injured, more by luck than by design. I muttered expletives about the mechanic, adjusted the brakes myself, and finished the shift without incident.

Management were onto the heating problem with the cast iron brake shoes long before this happened, and were in the process of changing them to fiber ones. The first trip with the fiber shoes was a bit cautious, but it did not have to be. The new brake shoes worked just fine. Still lots of heat, but nothing turned red hot or went on fire.

I HAD A LOT OF EXCITING RIDES while in The Half. One of them was as close to a fatality as it gets, but it was strict routine that caused it. For ventilating purposes, there was always a big wooden door on every level. It was supposed to be closed all the time, but obviously, had to be opened in order for trips to pass in and out. To open the door at these times, there was a guy called a "trapper." His job was to listen and watch for the trips, open the door for them, then close it when they went through. The Half had its door and its trapper. The door, in this case, was only about one trip length outside the launcher grade.

It was easy for a trapper to succumb to routine,

since there was absolutely nothing going on between trips, and if he happened to be a bit sleepy, he slept. If he wasn't sleepy, he probably would be before the shift was over. This trapper had slipped into that routine, and he was so used to it that he would get up and open the door at the very last few seconds. It is something like we all experience when we have to get up early. Sedated by sleep, we say: "Just a few more minutes..." and snooze a bit more. Well, the trapper probably heard the trip coming in the distance and said: "Just a few more seconds..." and dozed again.

When the trapper came to life, I was halfway down the launcher grade, myself a victim of routine, because I was just letting the thing roll, expecting the door to be open. Instead, I saw the trapper leap up, run into the middle of the road, and make for the door. There was just no way that guy was going to open that door before the diesel got there—as a matter of fact, he wasn't even going to *get* to the door!

I felt sick. I was going to kill a man! I let out one panic-stricken roar: "Don't try it!" At the very last second the trapper jumped off the road, abandoned his attempt, and POW!—the diesel hit the door. It opened, for sure, and it wouldn't be closing. I didn't know whether to stay on the diesel or jump off.

I didn't have to decide. In less than a second, the unhinged door went to the low side and was mangled by the diesel and full boxes. I didn't get a splinter. I maintained control over the trip and finished that run very much awake.

On the way back in, I stopped to talk to the trapper, who was now also very much awake. He had the mangled door clear of the road, and he was okay, but his day was about to take a bad turn. When the overman noticed it a bit windy inside, and found out why, he sent the trapper up.

THIS WAS ONE OF THE LAST TIMES an accident like this would have a chance to happen. Automatic doors were already in the plans. They would open when the diesel and boxes ran up on a rail-high ramp to which they were connected. They were the answer to management's ventilation problems. There were to be two of them on every level where coal was being hauled. When installed, they were about two to three hundred feet apart—far enough so that when a diesel and trip went through one door, it closed before the diesel got to the next door and opened that one. The idea was to have one closed door on the level *all* the time.

Once I got accustomed to their operation, the automatic doors provided me with a steady source of amusement. They were made to solve ventilation problems, but they could have been made to terrify miners, they did that so well. It took me quite a while to relax as a full trip from the launcher grade pushed me up to and through these things. They did not open until the diesel was about thirty feet away from them. There was a ramp rail just an inch or so above and tight against the rail the diesel rolled on, so that it was impossible for the wheels to miss that ramp as they rolled toward the doors. This ramp was connected to the doors by a lever system, so that the weight of the diesel or boxes running on the ramp would open the doors—and when the fifteen-ton diesel was speeding toward them, they opened—with a WHAM! Not once did they fail, but it took me a long time to trust them. They looked like a solid black wall, and for someone not used to them, they were uncomfortably close before they opened.

TOURS BY OFFICIALS were a fairly regular event in the coal mine. The miners did not always know who they were, what they were, or why they were, but they were. The Half had its share. This day three or four of them came down the wall and out The Half level. After they toured the wall and watched The Pig in operation, they asked the chute runner to leave half a box empty for them so they could get in it and ride out on the full trip. Usually, I was told these guys would be on the trip and that I should take it easy. Not this time. This was a younger group of officials.

They got in the half-empty box they had requested, but one of them came to the front of the trip and asked if it would be all right to ride on the front with me. I said: "Sure." This was not supposed to be allowed, but it was another "blind eye" thing. Lots of guys did ride with me—it was damn dusty at the back end of the trip.

As far as safety on the front end of the diesel was concerned, it was just as safe as anywhere else. The guy had enough bumper to sit on, and he could put one leg over the headlight, with the foot of his other leg resting on the "club"—the figure "8" link that coupled to the empty trips. Then he could wrap his arm around the back of the driver's seat. Unless he took a heart attack, he could not fall off. Even if he did take an attack, I could hold him on.

I coupled to the full trip, and got in the driver's seat. The young official got on beside me and we started out. I opened the throttle and let the transmission take the diesel and full trip to top speed in high gear. At top diesel speed, I could detect a bit of nervousness in the official, but he hid it well, shouting questions to me about the power of the diesel, how long I had had this job, and similar small talk. He seemed to have the idea that this was a nice, clean, interesting job that I had here. He was wearing a pleasant semi-relaxed smile, and really seemed to be enjoying the new experience, expecting it would be the same all the way out. No, it would not be the same all the way out!

At the beginning of the grades, the diesel made its customary downward dip, and I let it reach full downgrade diesel speed, then slipped the gearbox lever into neutral, closed the throttle, and reached for the Westinghouse. It wasn't diesel speed any more—it was gravity speed, and I put just a little less brake on than usual. Now the thing was moving!

At the bottom of the first steep grade, the rails were lighter and the road was bumpier. The diesel dipped and dove—not unlike a bucking bronco. The arch rails closed in and the roof was low. Tighter quarters made it seem like the diesel was approaching the sound barrier.

Since the diesel had first tipped downward and picked up speed, the official was noticeably quiet. The diesel took an especially violent dive to the high side at a bad joint, and the official shot a nervous glance at me, seeking assurance that this outfit was really under control. I was calm but the official was not, and he sure as hell was not relaxed. The pleasant smile was long since gone—replaced by wide-eyed semi-terror. His lips were pursed as if he were saying "Oooo." This guy was definitely not enjoying his experience any more.

I felt slightly sadistic. The trip was going about as

fast as it could and still be stopped at the outside end. The question was: "Was the last full trip still there?" Just in case it was, I relented and applied a little more brake pressure.

The official wanted the experience of what this trip-hauling part of coal mining was like. He was getting it, but he was surely reconsidering the decision he had made to ride up front. If I had any feelings of mercy—which I did not—it was too late anyway.

We were at the top of the launcher grade now. The diesel tipped downward again, and picked up extra speed. The official was now as tight as a fiddle string. I could feel his arm that was wrapped around the back of the driver's seat. Good thing the seat was made of quarter-inch steel plate. If not, the guy would have warped it, he was gripping it so tightly. The rails were clicking, the wheels were roaring, and the wind rushed past our faces. The official desperately wanted this trip to end. However, the worst was yet to come.

Here were the automatic doors! When he saw himself so quickly closing in on them, he lost all pretense of official authority. Both his knees lifted, and he assumed the fetal position. He was sure he was going to die! The doors did their usual thing—stayed closed until a person was absolutely certain they were going to be crushed to death—then WHAM!—they opened. When they did, the guy looked at me with wide, thankful eyes. He said something I couldn't hear, but I lip-read: "Holy shit!" He was uttering other sounds of relief that the doors had opened, then he looked out and there it was all over again—the second set of doors! He assumed the fetal position again, and the doors had just as much compassion as they had had the last time. When he was sure he was going to bc a mangled mess, they opened with the usual announcement: WHAM!

Again his thankful "Holy shit!"—but it was not over yet.

I looked out the level and saw what I did not want to see: the last full trip I had left there was still there! Geez! Now I was worried, and the official caught my concern. I turned my full attention to the Westinghouse air brake—applying maximum pressure and releasing it before the wheels locked. The Westinghouse emitted rapid and excited exhausts of compressed air, and the official was getting ready to assume the fetal position for the third time, when he sensed as I did, that this thing was going to stop before it hit the parked full trip. Stop it did, with about half a trip length to spare!

The official stepped off the front of the diesel and stood beside the smoking brake shoes. With his head shaking back and forth, he expressed to me a mixture of authority, admiration, and sympathy. He was sure I had my life on the line with every trip. With all the gratitude of one who was thankful to be spared from death, he told me that if there was ever anything he could do for me, or anything he could get for me, just to let him know. He was speaking as if he knew I would soon be dead, and he wanted to grant me a last wish.

He walked away without giving his name or phone number, but that didn't matter. We both knew he could do nothing to change The Half. The parked full trip that was so much of a concern just a minute ago was leaving for the surface. I thanked the official, threw the brake off again, and coasted to the mark where the full trip was supposed to stop.

# The Half

NOT LONG AFTER our baby died, Norma was called back to Eaton's. She had been head of the shoe department there and they missed her—for good reason. She was an excellent worker. They called her back for stock-taking, but kept her on after that was over. Her added income introduced a new possibility into our lives. We could not get enough backing to buy a house, but now we could get enough to build a house—in stages. We decided to do just that. My dad gave us enough land to build on. He told me he would show me how to build a house, but I would have to do most of the work, since he had a bad knee.

Norma and I looked forward to having a real house of our own—one where the eggs would not roll off the table, or the snow drift in on our bed. Life became more full and exciting as we worked together for something we both wanted—and needed. Norma was pregnant again.

Not often, but a scattered time, Norma and I would talk about the dangers of the coal mine, especially after the near-fatal accident Norma's brother had. I told Norma I was not on the wall any more, but worked all the time now on the arch-railed level. No danger here of getting caught, like Bobby, under a fall of stone. That was only partly true.

THERE WERE INDEED TIMES when I could have been very dead, or at least badly mangled. Not long after my trip with the official, I was again almost out to the beginning of the grades with a full trip. As I did every trip, I checked the air pressure gauges for the brakes. Then I let the diesel get to top speed as it started downgrade, slipped the gearbox into neutral, reached for the handle of the Westinghouse air brake, applied enough pressure to keep the boxes snug against the diesel, then looked out the level. This time, death looked back at me! There, smack in the middle of the road was a fall of stone and "lagging"— small, three-foot timber. The adrenaline outdid itself. I thought of Norma and our unborn child.

I rammed the air brake handle into emergency position—which locked the wheels and applied sand— then put one foot on the bumper, ready to jump off. But I hesitated. At this particular spot there was a mangled mess of discarded arch rails. I definitely did not want to jump into that—nor did I want to stay on the diesel and be impaled by a timber or torn apart in a pile-up. I didn't have to decide the lesser fate—the two-second hesitation was enough.

By that time the diesel had plowed *through* the stone and lagging. The locked wheels had pushed the debris away instead of running up on it and off the road. I could hardly keep track of what was happening. I was now on the outside of the fall of stone and still on the road! Aside from my wildly pounding heart, the only thing wrong was that the diesel's wheels were locked. I threw the brake off, which got the wheels turning again, then regained control over the trip which was only slightly over speed. I was trembling for the rest of the way out, but the ride was business as usual.

Another incident was not as frightful, but no less dangerous. Once again, I was a victim of sloppy maintenance. During what I thought was a routine haul with a full trip, trouble began to develop with the brakes. Every time I put them on with as much pressure as usual, the wheels locked. After two or three lock-ups, and the few seconds it took to throw the brake off and let the wheels turn again, the trip was going too fast. I was losing control. I could not put as much pressure as needed on the brakes—the wheels kept locking. The sanders were not working!

Nothing could be done about that now—I had to ride this trip through to the landing. My only option was to put as much pressure as I knew the wheels could take, and let the trip go. It was going too fast, but if I kept locking the wheels it would go even faster.

Complicating matters was the launcher grade still ahead. When I got to it, the trip was going too fast, but there was nothing I could do about it. By the time it got to the bottom of the grade and close to the first set of doors, it had approached runaway status. Then it started slowing down again, but not a hell of a lot. If the last full trip was not still on the landing, everything would be okay. I was almost there now. Too quickly I came to the doors and they opened—just a few feet more and—damn!—the last full trip was still there.

The diesel was still slowing down, but definitely not enough. I was going to ram the parked trip— hard—and I sure as hell wasn't staying on this thing. There was lots of room inside the landing to jump off the diesel, so I left the brake setting where it was and bailed off. I watched as the distance closed between the headlight and the shiny aluminum box of the parked trip, then BANG!—the collision. The mounds of coal on top of the moving trip kept going forward, spilling over between the boxes. The parked trip was driven several box lengths farther out the level, and the mounded coal on it stayed where it was while the boxes moved out from under the coal, again spilling it in between the boxes. Then all was quiet except for the rumbling engine a short distance away.

I walked out to the diesel. My lunch can was on the pavement beside the diesel, but it had not been run over, and the tea bottle was still intact! There was a lot of coal all over the diesel seat and on the road where it had been jolted off and between the boxes, but aside from that, everything was okay.

I coupled to the parked full trip and pulled it back in to the mark, uncoupled it and pushed the other full trip in a bit to the single road. Then I checked the sanders. I had guessed right—they were not working. Why? Some damn dummy had put wet sand in the sand boxes. Not only that, there was no fresh dry sand available.

I was fuming mad, and totally pissed off. Some stupid shithead had put my life in danger with more careless maintenance. I always checked the sand boxes before the shift began, but I never did put my hand in to feel the sand. That was going to change.

Once again, I was going to get a bit political. This was my life, and it was obvious that if I was to keep it, I would have to look out for myself. I decided there would be no more full trips until dry sand was available. I landed that trip, ordered dry sand, then went in with the empty trip. I left it on the spare road, told the chute runner to inform the overman I was going out to wait for dry sand, then left with the empty diesel. I knew my order for dry sand would receive moderate attention, but when the overman got on the phone with the news that the wall was tied up until dry sand arrived, *that* would get top priority.

The overman was not very pleased, but he was understanding. When I saw him personally, I did not receive so much as a dirty look for my decision to tie up the wall. However, for now, everything was on hold until dry sand arrived. I sat and waited.

It took close to an hour before the dry sand arrived. I filled the sand boxes, and the shift continued.

THE FULL TRIPS were the most challenging, exciting and dangerous. The empty ones were the most frustrating and, in an indirect way, probably more dangerous. After the first empty trip of each shift was taken in, the party was over. It was heat and smoke from then on.

On the way in with every empty trip, I had to stop at a cutoff at the inside of the landing to cool the engine down before starting up the grades. There was a water hose there. I would stick the hose into the radiator filler hole—there was never a cap on the radiator—start the water running, then race the engine. The water pump would quickly circulate cool water through the cooling system. When the temperature gauge showed 100 degrees or so, I would shut the water off, remove the hose, and start in.

The frustrating part was that the diesel was only over the first grade when the temperature gauge started touching the 212-degree mark again, and the engine started to billow thick, black smoke—so thick that I literally could not see the front end of the diesel fifteen feet away—even with the special highly polished reflector lamp. This continued for the rest of the way up the grades, the smoke getting thicker and the water getting hotter. I hated to breathe, but I had to. The temperature gauge was well over the 212-degree boiling point most of the time. Once the diesel and trip were over the grades, the smoke stopped, but then the transmission shifted into high gear, and the engine r.p.m. decreased to compensate for the higher gear.

Every single time the engine r.p.m. dropped like this, hot, steaming, boiling water shot straight up from the radiator filler opening, as if trying to blow a hole in the roof of the level. I couldn't do a thing about this, but I was not the least sympathetic towards the engine. In fact, I was totally ticked off, and muttered to myself: "Boil you gawd-damned smoke-spewing son-of-a-bitch bastard, boil!" and I jammed the already wide-open throttle as hard as I could against the throttle stop—expressing totally useless frustration at the machine that was filling my lungs with thick, black, oily, hot, diesel smoke. I never once thought about a filtered breathing mask—no one did in those days. To this day, especially when I puff so hard when doing so little, I wonder how much damage that smoke did to my lungs. The full trips didn't get me, but maybe the empty ones did.

ONE MONTH AFTER WE MOVED into our partly finished house, Noreen was born. What a doll! She was every parent's dream. A beautiful infant, and she had a good mix of smiles and tears. More: she slept most of the night.

Husband and wife roles were now expanded to father and mother. As our cultural conditioning determined, Norma and I did what was expected of us. I was a good provider and protector from the elements. Not a small task in the cold Cape Breton winters.

Most mornings, I was up at 5 A.M. to thaw out frozen water pipes with the naphtha torch, before going out on day shift. There was no basement under our partially finished house. I would crawl under the house in the frost, and play the torch on the copper pipes until the water started to flow. Then I would go to work. Norma would be up before it froze again.

Whatever broke, I was expected to fix it, and I did. The 1947 DeSoto was no exception. This provider role brought tremendous pressure with it! If we sacrificed to buy a part we could not afford, and somehow I ruined it, or that part did not fix the problem, I saw myself as a failure. I had caused hardship by losing the investment. It really hurt when Norma expected me to solve our problems, and I was unable to do so.

Norma was an excellent mother and housekeeper. Our house was always spotless, meals were always ready, clothes always washed, and Noreen perfectly cared for. There might have been women just as good as Norma, but there could be none better.

Unknown to both of us just yet, the seeds of lonesomeness and discontent were being sown. The irony was: the better we were at our separate gender roles, the more these seeds were being sown. The father and mother roles we lived so well were already beginning to separate us.

Most of the fault was mine. I never changed a diaper or comforted Noreen. That was Norma's job! I would enjoy Noreen's smiles and cute baby ways, but when she began to cry, I would quickly pass her to Norma. My time was spent on the house, the pit, the garage, and worse, hunting and fishing on weekends, leaving Norma alone with Noreen. Norma would ask: "Are you going hunting again?" I was, and the argument was on. Norma always gave in.

I stupidly found my recreation in the woods with my miner buddies instead of with Norma and our child. Norma had no recreation. She began to feel very shortchanged, and I did not give her feelings enough attention. In my ignorance, I thought I was being a good father, but I was only being a coal miner father— the kind I grew up with.

# 10

# The Quarter

AFTER TWO YEARS OR MORE in The Half, I got another nod. "We want you in 16 East." Adrenaline again! And again, for good reason. This was another "slant" level, but the main level part of it was even older than The Half—and the rails were lighter. This was the level on which Woody and I were given such a wild ride by the crazy donkey runner. I knew from experience: this place was steep!

The first time I went walking in here with Woody, I wasn't the least interested in how steep it was, even after the wild ride. Now, since I would have to let full trips out this level, not with the safety of a rope, but with the diesel on the front end of the trip, I was intensely interested in the grades.

My first impression, by sight, was: "Never!" A diesel wouldn't hold a full trip back on this level. This first impression was too close for comfort. A diesel *would* hold a full trip back on this level—just! There was no such thing, on the main level part of The Quarter, as choosing, even to a limited degree, how fast you would let the trip go. On this level, the full trip had to be under constant control, and the speed was always the same: slow! Not only that, but here in The Quarter a new element had to be introduced—ring sprags!

Ring sprags were simply a piece of round, hardened steel, one inch in diameter and about two feet long, with a ring on one end by which they could be held. After coming out of the slant, and before starting out the main level, I would stop the full trip and a guy would put one ring sprag between the spokes of four wheels on the full trip. Spragging those four wheels stopped them, and made them drag over the sanded rail, helping to hold the trip from gaining too much speed. This didn't do much for the wheels, but it did the trick. The diesel was then able to hold the full trip under control.

As a matter of fact, the diesel could stop the full trip on the main level, but only if the operator knew he had to do so. The ring sprags were necessary because of the steepness of the landing where the trip had to be stopped. There was a mini launcher grade at the inside of this landing. There was no room for error here. The trip had to be under full control at the top of this grade, and when the diesel and full trip started down this grade, it was at walking speed only—no more. The ring sprags provided this insurance.

Once stopped, the full trip had to be pushed back in about a foot, so the ring sprags could be removed. The diesel would have all it could do to move the full trip back that much. Then the landing tender would uncouple the diesel from the full trip. To keep the trip from moving once the diesel moved away, he put two or three wooden, triangular "chocks" against the wheels—just like a rock is put against a car tire to keep the car from moving.

Now, another obstacle had to be overcome. The diesel was in the outside part of the landing, called the "drift." It was the part where the level branched onto the main deep. The level here turned sharply left, and quickly up. The diesel, when uncoupled from the full trip, had to then go up the drift on the full road, and be switched to the empty road. The problem was that the drift was so steep above the switch, that it was not uncommon for the empty diesel to make two or three attempts to get above the switch, so it could be switched to the empty road.

I used the same technique as an airplane before takeoff. I had to leave the brakes on, open the throttle all the way and wait a few seconds, then throw off the brakes and apply sand. Hopefully, the diesel would roar far enough up the drift to pass the switch. If it did, it was still tricky, because the brakes had to be applied a second before the diesel stopped, so they would be completely on at full stop. If they were applied only when the diesel stopped, just the split-second before they gripped the wheels was enough to let the diesel move an inch or so back down. That was enough. If the diesel moved back down an inch or two, it slid all the way back down and rammed the full trip.

Even when it *was* stopped, it sometimes started back down anyway, just because of the steepness of the drift. Before shifting the switch to the empty road, the landing tender and I habitually waited a few seconds to see if the diesel would indeed stay where it was. It was crazy!

This drift, in all probability, was driven for small, wooden boxes. Here we have a fifteen-ton diesel locomotive on it! This very touchy situation was to be the reason for my first trip to the hospital.

ALL THIS WAS A CONSTANT SOURCE of anxiety and concern with every full trip, but inside, where the trip was loaded, it was even worse!

Once coupled to an empty trip, the diesel took it in the main level, but it did not go all the way in the main level. About half a mile in, it switched to the left, then went for another half mile in this branch off the main level, called the "slant." At the inside, coal-producing end of this slant, it was a diesel runner's nightmare. As usual, there was a spare road, like a siding on a regular railroad, where the empty trip waited until the full one went out.

From the inside of this spare road to the loading chute was where the nightmare was. I pushed the empty trip from this spare road to the loading chute. Once before, in The Half, I saw boxes disappear into the roof as they went up a very steep grade. Now, in The Quarter, was the worst situation I ever saw. Once off the spare road, and on the way in, three or four boxes was all that I could see. The other eleven or twelve were "up."

This place was so steep that if there were four or five boxes of timber on an empty trip, it was not uncommon for the diesel to spin its wheels while pushing the trip in, lose traction, and go back out by the run. Here is where the sanders tied in reverse saved the day. With sand, the trip could be stopped in half the length of itself, and another attempt be made to push it in.

The real nightmare, however, was on the way out!—trying to keep the full trip from going by the run on this grade. There was always an element of danger in a coal mine, and too often, it had its day and its way. But aside from the roof coming in on the wall, the actual coal mining dangers of explosion, fire, flooding, and gas were seldom given any thought by the ordinary miner. For the most part, this stuff was trusted to management, and as far as humanly possible, that trust was probably well founded.

However, when I was at this steep grade with a just-loaded full trip, with a low, narrow, cluttered level ahead of me, it was dangerous, and I was damned well scared. Every full trip from here was potential death or disaster. If the diesel got away on me, there were not that many places where there was room enough to jump off. And to jump off, then roll under the wheels would be like jumping from the frying pan into the fire. If I stayed on after losing control of the trip, would the other diesel be on the inside spare road switch? If it were—game over!

This diesel was definitely over-taxed, and my ability to compensate for this over-taxing was all that was between me and death—or someone else's death. Fact was: this was a fifteen-ton diesel with only four points of steel-to-steel contact where the wheels touched the rails. It should not, and could not, be trusted to keep control over fifteen full boxes of coal on these grades! Whoever had to control this weight with this machine was in danger.

It was so touchy that very often the diesel could hold only thirteen or fourteen of the fifteen boxes under the chute as they were getting loaded. The trip went by the run before it was fully loaded. Once on its way from the chute to the spare road, stopping it was out of the question. The best that could be hoped for was to keep it going slow enough so it could be stopped once it reached the spare road.

When the diesel first started in The Quarter, stopping on the spare road was not really a concern, because the diesel only took the empty trip to the spare road, and the full one from the spare road out to the landing. Haulage ropes took the trip from the spare road to the chute, and let the full one back out to the spare road.

Now, however, a new development: management decided to get rid of all rope haulages and use diesels only. This meant that the diesel had to pull the empty trip to the spare road, stop it there, go out the full road to the other end of the empty trip, then push the thing in under the chute. Then, the height of monotony: the diesel runner had to "spot" the trip in order to load it with coal—that is, move each box three or four times in response to a flashing red light used by the chute runner. One flash to start, another to stop. It was not uncommon to respond to 120 flashes per trip, not counting the double flashes which were the signal to push the trip in a little bit more when it had moved out too far.

But the major concern: while this trip was being loaded, another empty trip was being hauled in to the spare road with *another diesel! Two* diesels now on the level.

Stopping the full trip on the spare road became a major concern. The reason? The other diesel could be just coming onto the spare road with the empty trip, and in the process of switching from one end of the trip to the other, had to use the full road. This made it absolutely essential that the full trip coming from the chute be under such control that it could be stopped at the inside of the spare road.

This, however, was not something that could be guaranteed in The Quarter. It was always a variation of Russian Roulette, using diesels instead of bullets. Making it infinitely worse was that the outcoming diesel could not be seen from the spare road until it was down off the grade and on the flat—this would be a short fifty feet or so from the inside switch of the spare road.

The drift on the outside end of The Quarter was the reason I landed in the hospital. The steep grade on this inside, coal-producing end was the reason I left 12 Colliery. I would never forget 16¼ East.

NORMA AND I HAD LONG SINCE DECIDED we wanted two children. Two years after Noreen was born, that decision was realized. Bruce was born. Another boy, and Norma and I started to worry right away. Would he be the same as our first boy? We worried for a while. Bruce didn't cry as much as the first little guy, but he was a bit fussy. The first little guy could not take nourishment because of a throat restriction, but Bruce was taking nourishment. We began to relax a little more after each feeding. Finally, we were sure—Bruce was going to make it! That was definite relief, but Norma's job increased. Now she had two children to be left alone with on weekends.

My job looked pretty much the same to Norma, but in reality, it increased in tension as much as did Norma's—although completely unrelated. We were together, but we were alone. Norma was a mother with mother problems, and I was a father with father problems.

# 11

# The Beginning of the End

THE ACCIDENT THAT SENT ME to the hospital
happened when management first decided to get rid of
all haulage ropes and just use diesels. I was breaking
in a guy for the second diesel. We had just negotiated
a full trip out the level and onto the landing. I uncoupled the diesel from the full trip. Now, the new guy
had to get the diesel up the drift far enough so it could
be switched to the empty road. It took two or three attempts, and the new guy was having second thoughts.
He was not all that sure that he wanted to do this for a
steady job.

However, he finally got the diesel up the grade far
enough so that the switch could be shifted to the
empty road. I waited the few seconds to be sure the
diesel was going to stay there, then shifted the switch
to the empty road, and walked down to the first empty
box, getting ready to couple the diesel to it.

I was about to step between the couplings of the
parked full trip, then signal the new guy to let the diesel down from the drift—when BANG! No signal
needed. The diesel came down from the steep drift and
violently rammed the empty trip. Whether it started

140

down by itself, or the new guy released the brake a bit, the diesel came down out of control and slammed into the first empty box beside which I was walking.

I was slammed against the full box. I never felt so much pain in my life! From the waist down, it felt like boiling jelly, and I could hardly breathe. I was hanging by my hands from the top of the full box, unable to stand.

From out of nowhere came Jack, an old school acquaintance—the same guy who loaded the section of coal when I went to 19 East to run diesel. I told him: "I can't stand." Jack, with his arms under my armpits, said: "Just let yourself go," and he and another guy lowered me to the pavement, and sent for a stretcher.

I was sure I would never walk again, but after three or four days in the hospital, I was able to stand and begin walking. X-rays showed nothing broken— "crushed" was what the doctor told me.

When I got back, the guy I had been breaking in had decided this job was not for him, so they had got another fellow, Danny. By the time I returned, Danny really knew the level, and could be trusted to keep things under control. It was then that they started using the second diesel.

Things went well for a while, and would have kept going that way if it were not for Danny's decision to work only his eight hours. Danny was suffering from rheumatism, and also, he was not overly enthusiastic about hauling coal out of The Quarter to begin with. For whatever reason, Danny went home at home time whether the wall was cleaned off or not. That meant a replacement for him had to be brought in. It was then that the stakes went up for me.

I can't remember one replacement who was able

to hold the full trip under sufficient control from the chute to the spare road. This was no reflection on the replacement guy. Nobody could simply step in and do this job without some practice. The only reason I had not yet had an accident involving a replacement guy was that I had not yet been caught on the spare road when the replacement guy took the trip out from the chute. Again, it was Russian Roulette with diesels, and the diesel runners were lucky. That was soon to change.

IT WAS AN OVERTIME SHIFT and Danny had gone home. Another guy took his place. I waved a greeting to him as I passed him on the spare road on the way out with the full trip. The new guy went in with the empty trip, and I wondered—and worried. How will this guy do now when that trip is loaded, and he has to let it out?

I was determined to get to the landing and back with the empty as soon as possible, so I would be parked on the empty road and out of the way before the full one was loaded. This was not to be. I had to wait for empties. By the time they landed an empty trip from the main deep, and I started in with it, the trip under the chute could well have been loaded and on the way out. It was!

I came in the main level, then started nervously into the slant. I was expecting the worst, ready to bail off if I saw the other diesel coming towards me. I shut the diesel headlight off, took the lamp off my helmet, and shone it downward so it would be dark ahead, and I could better see if the other diesel headlight was coming at me.

I was halfway in—so far, so good—but then I saw

something almost as bad as another diesel headlight. I was driving through it—dust!—lots of dust! This dust had its own smell to it—not like the sharp, lively smell of fresh coal dust and blasting powder. This was an old, musty smell—like something had been disturbed that should not have been. This was the smell of fear—it always meant danger.

Since a roof cave-in that could make that much dust was highly unlikely on an arch-railed level, that dust could mean only one thing—a pile-up. The replacement guy must have lost control of the full trip.

I was on red alert now, cutting speed and watching for "whatever" before I ran into it. Where I could not see over the top of the diesel, I stopped, backed up to a clear spot, then got off and walked in the level a bit. Seeing nothing, I returned to the diesel and drove in farther.

I stopped again at the next low spot, and walked in the level some more. Since I had walked almost to the spare road now, I decided to go all the way to it. There it was! Right on the spare road.

Dear gawd! Even if I had been parked on the empty road, I would not have escaped. I was glad I had to wait for the empty trip. I never saw such a mess. The replacement guy must have lost control as soon as the diesel started down the first grade.

The diesel was now crossways on the spare road, and on its side. The first four or five boxes coupled to it were crisscross and also on their sides. Everything— diesel, boxes, and arch rails—were covered with a thick, dark grey rug of dust. The derailed diesel had broken the eight-inch air line, and this caused total dust.

Aside from my own diesel engine idling in the distance out the level, everything was quiet. There were dirty dark grey lumps all over the pavement.

For the first time in my life, I was afraid to look at something. I did not want to look at those head-sized lumps—afraid one of them would be wet: the replacement guy's head. I reluctantly checked them all. With relief, I noted that there were no wet ones.

The replacement guy's head was right where it belonged—on his shoulders. He had bailed off when he first started to lose control. After the trip piled up, he went to the phone and called the outside landing to have someone shut off the main line air valve. He was now back inside at the chute to alert the overman.

I did not blame the replacement guy. It was management. They never should have put a new guy in a situation like that. They were just too anxious to get the wall cleaned off, and in doing so, safety was compromised.

After this accident, I went political again, making a unilateral decision—one that I was going to tell management rather than ask them. This time, management turned out to be surprisingly cooperative. I informed management that I would no longer start in the slant with the empty trip until I had a phone call from the spare road inside telling me that the full trip was parked on the full road, and it was safe to come in. I wanted this phone call even when Danny, the regular guy, was on the other diesel. This would also work in Danny's favour, since there were times when both he and I were unable to stop the full trip inside the spare road. Even if the full trip came only four or five boxes past the inside switch, that was much too far if the other diesel happened to be on that switch.

This worked well. It was the overman himself

who made the phone calls from the spare road to the outside end of the slant. This procedure slowed production, but it was well worth it.

THE RUSSIAN ROULETTE DAYS were over, but not the hair-raising experiences caused by the grade from the chute to the spare road. It was one of these experiences that led to my last shift in 12 Colliery.

It was a night shift, and the wall was late cleaning off. As usual, Danny went home at home time. Again there was a replacement guy on the spare road with the empty trip when I went out with the full one. Worry time again, but this time was different.

The wall was tied up because of a broken cutting chain on the Dosco Miner. This would take about an hour to repair. That gave me plenty of time to get back in with the empty trip, park it, then go lie down in the "pigeon hole" safely out of the way. Pigeon holes were dug into the rib at several places along the level so that someone walking in or out the level could get safely out of the way if a trip were passing by. There was one of these at the outside end of the spare road. That's where I was.

It was a long time before the trip under the chute was loaded. I was half asleep when I heard a "click" on the rails. It was like when we were kids, and we used to put our ear to the rail to listen for a train coming in the distance. Only here, there was no need to put an ear to the rail. It was very quiet, and the clicks of the diesel going over the rail joints could be heard in the pigeon hole.

It used to be fun listening to the clicks when I was a kid, but these clicks I was hearing now filled me with terror! Something was very wrong. The clicks were way too close together. Three or four clicks followed the first one in quick succession, and immediately my heart started to pound.

The diesel had just started out, and already it was going too fast. Click, click, clickedy click, click—faster and louder the clicks came, and faster and louder my heart pounded. No doubt in my mind now—the replacement guy had lost control again.

At first, I simply sat tight. I was very excited now, but I decided to stay in the pigeon hole and let the trip roar by. But then I remembered that mangled mess of the last runaway trip I saw—diesel and boxes on their sides and crisscrossed over the spare road. I remembered as well the bad joint just inside the pigeon hole where I was.

I started to have second thoughts. If that thing jumped the road at the bad joint, it would pile up right at the pigeon hole. It would certainly break the main air line, creating a choking dust. And it would probably also break the 500-volt armoured cable, making a flash big enough to easily ignite the dust. In the middle of it all, I would be trapped in this pigeon hole.

Those clicks were a loud rattle now, and were accompanied by a commanding rumble.

I panicked! There was another pigeon hole just a short way out the level. I thought it would be safer. It was stupid, but I did it. I bolted out of that pigeon hole and ran for the other one farther out the level. I made it in time, but as I turned to go into the "safer" pigeon hole, I slipped and fell right in the middle of the road.

The runaway diesel and full trip did not jump the road at the bad joint. I looked up from between the rails and there was the headlight of the pounding, rocking diesel, driven like a javelin by the full trip.

There was no one on it! The replacement guy had bailed off.

The diesel was no more than twenty feet away. I was sure I was finished—my legs were like rubber—but I got my feet under me again and literally dove for the pigeon hole. All of me made it except my right foot. The diesel hit it and broke it, but I could not have cared less about a broken foot. I should have been very mangled and very dead. My foot was hurting and my heart was pounding, but I was very happy. I was still alive.

That was it! Now I really went political! I made a decision, and I knew it was final as soon as I made it. Regardless of what management might say, I was never going to operate a diesel again in The Quarter. As a matter of fact, if I could get out of 12 Colliery completely, I would. As soon as I had a walking cast on my foot, I hobbled to the manager's office and asked for a transfer to 18 Colliery. I was certain I would not get it, but I applied anyway.

The next payday, I was at the pay office just outside the wash house. I picked up my envelope and was in my car ready to leave when the production overman for The Quarter got in and sat beside me. He had heard that I had asked for a transfer. He had come to get me to change my mind, and return to the diesel in The Quarter. This was an honour to my worth, and much appreciated, but there was to be no change of mind. Even if I did not get the transfer, I would not be going back on the diesel in The Quarter.

For me it was a life-or-death decision. I was sure that it was only a matter of time before I would be seriously hurt or killed. I never asked the overman why he kept putting a replacement guy on the other diesel when he knew it was likely a new guy could not control the trip. It would take a little longer, but it would be much safer to use my diesel alone when Danny went home. I never asked, because it didn't matter any more. The Quarter was history now!

I WAS DOUBLY CERTAIN I would not get a transfer, because a member of management wanted me to stay in 12 Colliery. I was pleasantly surprised, however, to find out that I was wrong. I did get the transfer to 18 Colliery.

It took six weeks for my foot to heal. When it did, I started in 18 Colliery as landing tender on the main deep landing. My father was on the main hoist on the surface on one shift, and my brother was on the same hoist on the next shift. They were landing empty trips to me and I was hooking on the full trips that they hoisted to the surface. I was working with family now. Things were looking up.

THE LANDING TENDER JOB was a good one, but it wasn't long before management at 18 Colliery told me not to get used to it, because I was going back on the diesel again. Sure enough, a week or so later, I was told to go to 4 West on the diesel. I knew in advance that there were no dangerously steep grades on the levels in 18 Colliery, so I was glad to get back on the diesel without having to worry if I would be killed or not. I accepted my new diesel-running duties with pleasure. The overman was good, and so was the level. It wasn't long before I was enjoying a good job on a level almost as good as 19 East in 12 Colliery.

However, something had changed.

The original satisfaction with my coal miner identity—felt on my first shift in 15 East in 12 Colliery—

had long since vanished. That began as early as my pan-shifting days. The possibility that I would have to spend my wage-earning days crawling around in coal mine clutter, and heaving 200-pound pans while on my knees, gave me second thoughts about being a coal miner for the rest of my working days. The gob was a change, but it wasn't long before it became very monotonous. Now this job on the diesel was outdoing the gob when it came to monotony.

This business of "spotting" the boxes with the diesel was a complete drag. I had to move the boxes for the chute runner to fill them with coal. Watching a red light flash more than 120 times a trip was not all that exciting. As diesel runner I had to keep staring at the light, or at least very close to it, for the entire time the trip was being loaded. If I missed one flash, and did not move the trip, the chute runner went ballistic—and for good reason—the coal would be spilling all over the already-filled box, and onto the road, making for the possibility that the boxes would derail when they ran up on the spillage.

Even at six boxes away, and with the engine running, I often heard the chute runner screaming and cursing at me because I missed a signal to move the trip. If I blinked my eyes slowly at the same instant the red light blinked, I would not see it!

It was not uncommon for the diesel and chute runners to be at each other's throats for the entire shift. Sometimes the chute runner, trying to get the diesel runner's goat, would let the trip go out a few feet too far, then give two flashes, commanding the diesel runner to push the trip back in. The diesel runner, after spotting boxes for a year or more, knew when the chute runner did this, and would retaliate by not pushing the boxes back in, or by pushing them very, very slowly, or by pushing them in too far. Then the war was on!

I was no stranger to these anger-filled times. Bottom line was: running diesel in 18 Colliery had become very monotonous and very frustrating.

IT WAS DURING these monotonous days that I started working my way out of the coal mine. It was becoming more and more obvious that I was not going to be a coal miner for the rest of my working days. I was glad to get the job in the first place because it was the means by which I was able to carve out a place for myself under the sun. I got married, and built a house, and a backyard garage where I repaired cars. From this home base, I was able to go hunting and fishing with my miner buddies—a hobby I enjoyed too much as far as Norma was concerned.

Yeah, something was happening. During a rain- or snowstorm, I used to go from window to window in my very own house, taking in as much of the storm as I could. I was in the "nest" I had built. It felt good, but now I was beginning to ask: "Is this all? Is this nest to be the reason for life?"

The house was not important enough to satisfy the purpose of life itself. The same thing was happening with the garage where I used to enjoy working on cars. And the hunting and fishing: I waited for hunting and fishing seasons like a child waiting for Santa Claus. Now that was fading as well.

The meaning was draining out of the life I had made for myself. If I were going to do anything more with my life, I had better get at it soon. I was in my early thirties, and not getting any younger.

## The Beginning of the End

BOTH NORMA AND I had achieved coal mining society gender-role expectations—we had done well—too well! As a father and family man, I felt I was a model—that is as far as my dumb role expectations went. I was a good provider and an authority figure. But that was not the father and family man that my family actually needed.

The kids were "to be seen and not heard." I had no patience with their whining and fighting. They were to do as they were told, and that was it! No such thing as dialogue with them.

As a husband, I was no better. When I came home from work and had supper, the rest of the day was mine—as were the weekends. I was in the garage on weekdays after work, and hunting or fishing on the weekends. Norma was left on her own with the kids. She had little or no support from me.

All this was too much for Norma. She was coming to her wits' end. Her nerves were shot. She expected more of life as a married woman; now she was afraid that this was "it." Things were not going to get any better. She cried. She had done—and was doing—her level best. She was more than living up to the coal mining society's expectations. But that society was not living up to her expectations. When she looked at her life and asked: "Is this all? Keep house, raise kids, pay bills....?" The hard answer was: "Yes!" She felt trapped.

And I felt trapped. It took me much longer, but I felt just as trapped as Norma. The sad part of it was, we did not feel trapped together—as a team. We were trapped in our own expectations—expectations that separated men and women. The common bond of coal mining society that had brought us together was now threatening to tear us apart. It was a god with clay feet.

# 12

# Bye-Bye
# Coal Mine

I REMEMBERED MY SCHOOL DAYS, and how I blew my Grade 11 in the poolroom. Now I saw my mistake. But even if I had known this was to happen—that I'd feel that I had hit a dead end—I would have quit school anyway. The hard reality was that when I had no responsibilities, and the chance to make something of my life, I did not know what to make of it. I had had no aspirations beyond the pit!

Now, however, I aspired to an education and a professional occupation. But now I had economic responsibilities: house and car payments, and the maintenance of a family. We had two lovely children that had to be cared for. In the face of that, I started studying anyway.

I was convinced that a person could get nowhere without a Grade 11 education. So I decided to correct that mistake. I applied for correspondence courses available from the province at no cost. But provincial exams had to be written at a high school. This was the worst part: writing the exams in the high school with the other, younger students. It was quite a scene—a 32-year-old coal miner sitting in a room full of teenagers. But none of the teenagers seemed to notice—they were too uptight themselves at exam time.

It took three years, but I did it. I passed all the exams and received my Grade 11 diploma—sixteen years late. There was no graduation prom or any ceremony whatever. No one seemed to notice. But no high school graduate could have been more pleased than I was. As it turned out, Grade 11 was the smallest hurdle. I still had a family to maintain and payments to make. A college education was necessary for any professional occupation, but how in hell could I ever quit the pit and go to college? It was economic madness even to think of it.

BUT THINK OF IT I DID. As a matter of fact, I could not stop thinking of it. Norma knew what I was thinking, but we never discussed it seriously, because it seemed like such an impossibility. Would any college accept me? Word had it that a person went from school to college, not from a coal mine to college. Sixteen years was a long time to be out of the education system. Was it possible for a person to get back in now? I asked around, and found out about student loans, bursaries and grants.

Also: Norma's mother was a widow now, living alone. If we sold our house, we could move in with her. She would love to have us, and we would have a rent-free place to live while I was studying. Things were looking up. This college idea might not be so impossible after all.

The clincher came on night shift in 4 West in 18 Colliery. As usual, I was thinking about college. As usual, the same economic madness came to mind. Not as usual, however, was the shot of adrenaline to my stomach. I became extremely excited, and at the same time, sensed that this college idea was a definite possibility. It was not like I was making up my mind. It was like this excitement made up my mind for me. From that instant on, there was no turning back. I knew somehow I was going to "go for it."

I didn't ask Norma—I told her. She was disappointed because we had not really talked it over before this sudden announcement. However, she was not at all against the idea! As a matter of fact, she was quietly pleased. Worried, but pleased. Worried, because she was the one who paid the bills. Pleased, because she liked the idea of leaving behind her this life as a coal miner's wife. Once she got over the initial shock, she was one hundred percent behind me, and ready to go. I was sure she would follow me into hell. As a matter of fact, she had. Now, hopefully, she would follow me out!

WHEN WE WERE READY to make the move, there was no one to follow. I had no solid idea of where to start. I still did not know if a coal miner sixteen years out of school would be accepted into college. The time had come to find out .

It was August 1—Miners' Vacation time. We loaded up the old DeSoto, put the kids in the back seat with instructions to behave, and headed for Mount Allison University in Sackville, New Brunswick. We were so out of touch, we never once thought about any college being already full. This one was, and a simple long distance telephone call would have saved us the five-hour trip. Geez!

All was not lost, however. Talking to the registrar, I asked about my chances of getting into any college. The registrar saw no reason why I could not be accepted. My hopes skyrocketed. The registrar then suggested that I try Dalhousie University in Halifax.

I made a beeline for a public telephone on the street in front of Mount Allison. I called Dalhousie University and asked for the registrar. I got to the point. I asked if they were still taking students. The registrar was equally to the point, and said: "Yes." Now the adrenaline was like a river. We still had time to get to Halifax before 5 P.M.—and we did!

Sitting across from the Dalhousie registrar, I proudly presented my Grade 11 graduation certificate and marks. The registrar began shaking his head. Bottom line was: I would not be accepted at Dalhousie University. In my ignorance, I knew nothing about higher standards in some colleges than in others. I thought a college was a college. My heart sank. It was all over!

But as fast as my heart sank, it skyrocketed again. The registrar said: "Try St. Mary's. They have a mature matriculation clause in their constitution that allows for older students." I did not know what a constitution was, but I liked the sound of "mature matriculation," and the words "older students" were the most hopeful words I had heard to date.

Early next morning, I went to St. Mary's University. Everyone stayed in the car while I went in, semi-dejected and confused. I came out ecstatic! The St. Mary's registrar promised me that they would accept me—but on finding out where I lived, the registrar suggested I try St. Francis Xavier in Sydney, Cape Breton, since they also had a mature matriculation clause in their constitution.

I had never seriously considered St. Francis Xavier. As far as I was concerned, a person could only get part of a degree there—something like night classes. Not so! Fact was: two years at St. F.X. in Sydney, and then two years at St. F.X. in Antigonish, were enough for a degree as good as any other college's. Once the registrar at St. Mary's explained this to me, I was hell-bent for Sydney.

Poor Norma, Noreen and Bruce. I went ballistic! I was a pressure cooker. When we stopped for dinner the kids, young as they were, sensed their father's excitement and burning desire to get to Sydney. They didn't *dare* pick at their food, or fuss around. They were wide-eyed and wondering, hoping they would soon be back home and relaxed. I drove a little too fast, but we made it easily.

Three P.M. that same day: I was sitting across from Father Campbell, the principal of St. Francis Xavier in Sydney. Father Campbell gave me the same assurance as the registrar at St. Mary's. I would be given the chance I wanted here at St. F.X.—just twenty minutes from home. Wow!

I applied, and was accepted, for entry into St. F.X. right then and there.

The tension was over! Now we knew. Yes, a coal miner could get into college after being out of school for sixteen years. Not only that, but I could stay at my mother-in-law's place and go to college from there—a fact that would save us a lot of financial anxiety. We also found out that, yes, a person can quit work for full-time study and still support a family. There were other jobs besides mining coal, and I would find one.

Norma would also get part-time work while her mother looked after the children. Things were looking up. Our life together was now extremely exciting. All we could talk about was the new life that was unfolding, and how we would manage.

FRIDAY WAS TO BE my last shift. I thought: "Four years from now, what the hell difference will one shift make?" I said: "I am not going to work tonight!" and gave my full lunch can to a miner friend, then sat back with Norma to look at our future. Monday, I would be in college. What a switch!

My first day in class was almost as much a heart thumper as a runaway trip on the diesel. I was in a clean, bright classroom—taking notes with thirty or forty other students. Geez! It was pure, exciting adventure—and it stayed that way! This was not hard to get used to! I had to put on "good" clothes to go to "work." On the first day, walking down George Street, I saw a cluster of leaves blowing in the wind. I thought: "These leaves and me—together—on day shift!" Leaves were not supposed to be part of my working day.

The worst thing I feared now was that the professors would throw something at me that I could not understand. Was my brain still able to function, especially at college level? Yes, it was able. I made the dean's list every year, and graduated from St. F.X. in Antigonish in 1969.

For me, the coal mine was history.

# Epilogue

THEY CALL IT "Colliery Lands Park" now—where 12 and 16 Collieries used to be in New Waterford. They made a little lake there, and put trout in it. There is a wall monument to 307 miners who died here and at other pits. The grass is green and well kept, as are the trees and flowers. There are picnic tables with little roofs over them where a person can sit—and remember. A few coal boxes and some man rakes sit quietly by, the elements turning them into rusting and rotting relics.

This used to be a very busy place. Those man rakes are reminders of the mad stampede of men from this pithead memorial to the wash house. The coal boxes speak of the rattle and roar they made as they went down empty, fifteen at a time, changing to a muffled rumble when they came up full, streaking coal dust behind them.

No one would know now where the pulley is that squealed like a blackbird. It has no door now, and the door has no wash house. It is all gone. Beautiful memories are all that remain. Even the painful ones bring a tender smile—and over all, there is a satisfying sense of accomplishment.

**Rennie MacKenzie driving a diesel in Number 12 Colliery:** "You can see a bit of the trip there. Those are aluminum boxes full of coal. But this would be a good part of the level. Here you'd have more room. You're getting close to the landing there. Another trip length and you'd be on the landing."

**Below: "By golly—*that's* a haulage road.** That's more like what the diesel would be going through. That stuff. They don't show you those pictures.... I don't know how come they took that. Usually they don't take pictures like that.

"Now you imagine the diesels hitting in there. This is the kind of place that you'd have to go through slowly to find out if the diesel would fit through. And one of these arch rails'd be bent too close, you know.... That's the lagging in behind them. And the wood going across is the booms. And that roof is cracking. Eventually they'll go right in with the arch rails and this place will become part of the

main haulage road. Those booms'll come right down after a while and they'll have to take stone out, make more room. That's what you call 'brushing.'

"The chuck blocks are just tossed aside there. This is the kind of thing that you'd have to take the diesel through. Oh yeah, she's pretty tight in spots. Not the whole level'd be like that but...half of it. And where the mining's being done— that'd be further inside, in that dark. It'd be inside where you can't see there. This would be the outside end. By golly, that's quite an amazing picture."

**The man at the left is carrying new chuck blocks.**

**Below: A built chuck.** That chuck is one of many holding up the roof. Behind it you can see the rubble where the gob has been cut and has fallen in. That is, the timber in the gob has been cut and the roof has fallen down into the space from which the coal has been mined and removed. The coal face is at the back of the person taking the photo.

"Underneath the shaker pan [running across the photo] can be seen the two-inch steel pipeline for compressed air. The air drives the jackhammers and the pan engine and the Samson machine. One of the pan bolts can be seen as well. There's another bolt to be removed on the gob side in order to shift the pans. To get at that bolt you've got to get over on the other side and, see, you'll have a bit of a problem. Because that chuck is going to be close; the pipeline is going to be against the bolt over on the other side; so you're going to be cursing and growling and kicking and snarling and crying.... And there's 21 of them on one pan line—21 to 25. And at the top of the chuck, there's a wedge that looks like a crushed newspaper. That's a piece of timber that's used for a wedge. See, there wasn't enough room for another block on top before it hit the roof. So you had to put something smaller in there. When that piece of timber went in there, it was round." [See Chapter 4.]

**Above: "That's a Samson machine.** It's undercutting the coal. The Samson is like a great big chain saw, really, sawing a four-inch cut under there. Four inch by four-and-a-half feet. Or five feet. It varied in different pits. Down the wall it goes. They have a rope—and it's down the wall, and it's hooked onto a timber. They jam a timber against the roof at an angle. And they hook the rope on the bottom of the timber so the harder you pull on the rope, the more it jams the timber into the roof. So it anchors this thing. And the Samson then pulls itself along the rope, cutting as it goes."

**Right: "The shotfirer is using a cleaner**—that's got a little spoon thing on the end of it. Puts it in there and turns it down, then he hauls the duff out of the hole. Cleans it out. Then he puts the powder in. He's wearing a Davey safety lamp. Most of the guys called it a glimmer. Like I say, if that's all you had, you called it worse than that, because there's not much light comes off it. But that checks for gas. You wouldn't fire a shot if there was gas present...."

**Right: "That's the stemmer he's using there.** He'll push that right in to the back of the hole. He'll hold onto those two wires and they'll trail right through to the back of the hole. Then he'll hook his cable onto those. He's got a little dynamo on his belt. He'll go up the wall one way, and the guy who's loading the section will go the other way and just shout, 'Fire!' And then he'll come down on that dynamo and give her a twist and it will go WOOMP, and the coal comes down."

**"There's the automatic doors—oh, man.** They scared a lot of guys, I'll tell you that. Those things are kept closed. They're partially open there in the picture. But when you're coming at them, it just looks like you're going to run into a wall. And you're coming at them kind of fast...." [See Chapter 9]

**Below: The Dosco Continuous Miner**

The man holding the chuck blocks was photographed by Owen Fitzgerald—courtesy Beaton Institute, UCCB. All other photos in this section are by Leslie Shedden. Our thanks to Cyril MacDonald, Glace Bay, for permission to offer Shedden's photographs. Many more can be seen in *Mining Photographs and Other Pictures, 1948-1968.*

# Dominion Number 12 Colliery
# New Waterford

WHERE COLLIERY LANDS PARK NOW STANDS, work began in 12 Colliery in 1908, and New Waterford grew up with it. The earliest levels were worked as room-and-pillar, and the newer, deeper mine used long-wall methods as the colliery became more and more mechanized, introducing the diesel, the Dosco Continuous Miner, new roof support systems and, eventually, the Anderton Shearer. Number 12 was always noted as a great producer.

Considered a gassy mine, 12 Colliery was the site of the single greatest loss of life in a Cape Breton mine disaster. An explosion in 1917 took 65 lives (63 men and boys, and two more men who attempted rescues and were overcome by afterdamp gas). Voices of people who witnessed that explosion and the aftermath are included in "Mine Explosion in New Waterford, 1917," in *Cape Breton's Magazine* Number 21, 1978.

According to Paul MacEwan's *Miners and Steelworkers*, the coroner's jury found "the company officials guilty of gross neglect." A Department of Mines inquiry also accused the company, company officials and the provincial deputy inspector of mines of responsibility for the deaths. "A period of government and judicial silence" followed, until the miners "passed a resolution binding union members to strike every Wednesday and Saturday until the matter was brought into the courts. A Grand Jury of the Supreme Court of Nova Scotia was hastily convened at Sydney, and three officials were indicted for manslaughter. The Dominion Coal Company was also indicted, as a corporate body, for causing 'very grievous bodily harm' to its employees."

When the case came up again—October 28, 1918—"a new Supreme Court Judge, Mr. Justice Mellish, was in charge." Before his appointment, "he had been a member of the law firm acting as the company's chief solicitors, and had personally prepared the defence for the Company and its three officials. For three days, Crown Prosecutor Carroll presented his evidence. [Then] Mr. Justice Mellish directed that the case be withdrawn from the jury, as he did not think that 'there was enough evidence to warrant considering it.' When Mr. Carroll raised objection to Mr. Mellish's directions, '[Mellish] directed that the jury return a verdict of not guilty,' which the jury did without so much as leaving the jury box."

There is a memorial to the 1917 Explosion on Plummer Avenue in New Waterford. It lists the names of those who died, and at the top stands a remarkable statue of the shotfirer, John D. MacKay. These names are included in another memorial erected in Colliery Lands Park, honouring all the men who have died in Cape Breton mines.

Fire, falls, and especially gas continued to plague Number 12. For example, fire stopped work in 1943. The mine was sealed and water was let in through the air lines, dousing the fire. Two men died. In 1960 a runaway trip of mine cars caused a spark that set off a fire which idled the mine for over a week. There was no loss of life that time.

On March 2, 1973, Cape Breton Development Corporation president Tom Kent sent a letter in praise of Number 12's best per-man production effort in ten years. They had produced close to 5000 tons of coal in two days, well over four tons per man, exceeding production goals for the industry that year. The *Cape Breton Post*, March 3, 1973: "Number 12 Colliery, marked for closure in DEVCO's phase-down program, dramatically reversed its fortunes a year ago after officials of the United Mine Workers suggested production revert to a piecework system which was abolished in 1969. Under the revived piecework policy [known by miners as 'taskwork'], groups of miners are given specific assignments at the start of their shifts and are free to go home when they are finished. Productivity shot upwards shortly after the system was introduced on one wall and it was later extended to the whole mine.... Mr. Kent [said] the New Waterford feat was 'an encouraging omen' that long-term goals for the industry are attainable...."

Just three days later—March 5, 1973—there was another gas explosion and fire in Number 12, between 19 and 15 East Levels. *Cape Breton Post*: "The fire broke out when an empty trip jumped the rails around 19 East section on the Second Deep. The derailment caused a full trip further up the deep to go on the run, piling up on top of the empties and bringing down sections of the roof...."

DEVCO's engineering director, Donald McFadgen, age 47, died of a heart attack while inspecting the fire. And 28-year-old Earl Leadbeater became separated from fellow miners heading for the surface; his body was never recovered.

Though temporarily sealed, the mine continued to burn, with gas and water accumulating in the old workings. By February 25, 1975, the mine gas was bled off, the seals were made permanent, and the mine was allowed to flood with water. A gravestone was placed at the entrance to the mine in memory of Earl Leadbeater. Number 12 was through.

**CONTINUED ON NEXT PAGE**